Unlocking the Future

Developing new lifestyles with people who have complex disabilities

St cc Development (3266).

Unlocking the Future

Developing new lifestyles with people who have complex disabilities

Edited by Barbara McIntosh and Andrea Whittaker

Published by
King's Fund Publishing
11–13 Cavendish Square
London W1M 0AN

© King's Fund 2000

First published 2000

ISBN 1 85717 400 3

A CIP catalogue record for this book is available from the British Library

Available from:

King's Fund Bookshop
11–13 Cavendish Square
London
W1M 0AN

Tel: 020 7307 2591
Fax: 020 7307 2801

Printed and bound in Great Britain

Typeset by Peter Powell Origination & Print Limited

Contents

Preface

Introduction

The Changing Days work started in December 1994 as a three-year project to develop better day opportunities for people with learning difficulties. In the course of those three years we realised that one group of people was generally getting left out of new opportunities, and that was people with very complex needs. We were fortunate in obtaining funding from Lloyds/TSB for a further two years' work, to look specifically at how that group of people might be supported to have the same range of opportunities in the community as their more able peers.

Throughout the five years of the project the work has been based on the belief that:

- *people with learning difficulties have the ability to become full members of their local communities*
- *better daytime opportunities can be achieved by working in partnership with users, carers and staff in planning and shaping the future*
- *the future for people with learning difficulties should be away from segregated day centres and building-based services towards being given support to participate in ordinary activities in the community*
- *the emphasis should be on developing adult education, employment and meaningful leisure pursuits outside segregated services.* (*Changing Days*, 1996)

The development sites

We worked with three development sites:

Horizon NHS Trust (Harperbury Hospital), Harper Lane, near Shenley, Radlett, Herts WD7 9HQ. Tel: 01923 854 861; fax: 01923 853 246

Knowsley Social Services, Service Provision Division, Municipal Buildings, Cherryfield Drive, Kirby, Merseyside L32 1TX. Tel: 0151 443 4197; fax: 0151 443 4210

Newham Social Services, Broadway House, 322 High Street, London E15 1AJ. Tel: 020 8519 5454; fax: 020 8557 8755

Definitions

By people with complex needs we mean:

> *People with learning disabilities who have one or more of the following additional support needs – physical, sensory or communication impairment, mental health needs or behaviour which challenges people and services – or any combination of these factors. Because of their multiple needs they may have been excluded or have had reduced opportunities for activities, roles and types of relationships which others enjoy and that would enhance their quality of life.* (Developed by Knowsley Social Services.)

The terms 'learning difficulties' and 'learning disabilities' are used interchangeably.

Linking with earlier work

This book describes the results of the past two years' work and the lessons learned. It also includes contributions from people who have not been directly involved in the project but whose related experience we believe will be valuable to readers.

The book is the last of four publications that have resulted from the Changing Days work.

The first publication, *Changing Days,* brought together current ideas and practice on how best to achieve better day opportunities for people with learning difficulties. The second publication, *Days of Change,* builds on those ideas and records the experience gained through working with five development sites. It describes the lessons learned about how to achieve changes in the lives of individuals and what organisational changes are needed to make this happen.

An underlying principle in all our work has been to directly involve people with learning difficulties throughout the work. The third publication, *Changing our Days*, reflects this. It is a reproduction of the easy-to-read version of *Changing Days*, specifically written for people with learning difficulties, with the addition of Ideas for Action and an audio CD.

In this latest publication, we have tried to avoid unnecessary repetition of material from the first two books. Making the right decisions in this regard has not been easy, as the earlier material is still necessary to gain the best understanding of what is required to achieve positive results. For example, the basic steps necessary to achieve organisational change are still the same – from creating the vision right through to monitoring and evaluating changes in people's lives (see Appendix 1). The detailed ways of working with parents and carers (see 'Involving parents and families', Chapter 9 of *Days of Change*) remain true. The crucial importance of community building and how it might be achieved applies as much to people with complex needs as to people who are more able (see 'Getting a life, not a building' and 'Creating inclusive communities', Chapters 5 and 6 of *Days of Change*). We would therefore recommend that readers keep to hand copies of the first two books to use in conjunction with this volume.

Readership

As with the first two publications, this book is written particularly for managers, commissioners and providers who are responsible for developing day opportunities for men and women with learning difficulties. However, it is designed to be helpful also to anyone involved in supporting people to improve their lives, including people who use services and their families. We hope the easy-to-read section will be particularly useful for user committees and self-advocacy groups working with professionals to change services.

Suggestions on how to use this book

Unlocking the Future begins with an easy-to-read summary of the main text and ends with the Personal Planning Book used during the person-centred planning process. This handbook was developed largely from material already being used in the Changing Days sites, which we adapted and added to as experience suggested. We hope readers will find it useful in working out their own ways of supporting each individual to have his/her own personal planning record. We suggest that it be photocopied, enlarged to A4 size and used in a loose-leaf format.

Each chapter focuses on a specific area, giving practical information to managers and others in a position to make change happen. The chapters are arranged to highlight certain aspects of the work that we feel are crucially important for success. The early chapters concentrate on individuals and their lives – how to get to know someone with complex disabilities and what it might take to understand how she/he communicates and relates to the world. We believe that this is essential knowledge for everyone, not just frontline staff. Only when managers and others responsible for planning, delivering and monitoring services understand the importance of this starting point can they go on to make appropriate changes to the system. Later chapters consider ways of achieving more individual lifestyles and the processes that are necessary to create a truly person-centred service that will result in better quality lives for people with complex disabilities.

Barbara McIntosh
Andrea Whittaker
Changing Days Team

Acknowledgements

This book has come about through the combined efforts of the contributors listed on pages xii–xiv. We are very grateful to all these people for contributing their time, knowledge and experience so generously. We are also grateful to the contributors for their kind permission to reproduce the stories and case studies to be found throughout this book.

We want to thank also Janice Robinson, Director of the Community Care Programme at the King's Fund and Simon Whitehead, Deputy Director of the National Development Team, for their advice and support.

Particular thanks go to all the people in the development sites – people with learning difficulties, their parents and carers and staff at all levels. We have been impressed – and greatly supported in our work – by the enthusiasm, energy and commitment shown by so many people. As well as working together on some of the many challenges, it has been a particular pleasure to get to know and share in the development and successes – however small – of individual people as they move forward to a better quality future.

Thanks also to Mark Wilson, Managing Editor, Minuche Mazumdar, Design Manager, and Peter and Matt Powell for typesetting this volume.

Contributors

Person-centred planning

Angela Cole   Freelance Consultant, 40 King Street, Maldon, Essex CM9 5DY. Tel: 01621 857 819

Barbara McIntosh   Community Care Development Centre, 157–168 Blackfriars Road, London SE1 8EZ. Tel: 020 7928 7994; fax: 020 7928 4101

Andrea Whittaker   9 Stanhope Avenue, London N3 3LX. Tel/fax: 020 8346 7325

Communication

Phoebe Caldwell   Beechstones Barn, Mount Pleasant, High Bentham, Lancaster LA27 7A. Tel: 01524 261 661

John Ladle   Acting Up, 90 de Beauvoir Road, London N1 4EN. Tel: 020 7275 9173; fax: 020 7254 8990

Lyn Rucker   Lead Consultant, National Development Team, PO Box 70, Herington, KS USA 67449. Tel: 0161 228 7055 (UK contact); e-mail: rpaltd@aol.com

Health and primary care

Peter Hall   Physical Health Care, Horizon NHS Trust, Harperbury Hospital, Harper Lane, Shenley, nr Radlett, Herts. WD7 9HQ. Tel: 01923 854 861; fax: 01923 855 909

Education

Caroline Allen   Principal, Orchard Hill College of Further Education,
6 Elm Avenue, Orchard Hill, Fountain Drive,
Carshalton, Surrey SM5 4NR.
Tel: 020 8770 8125; fax: 020 8642 3763

Transition

Liz Maudslay   SKILL, 336 Brixton Road, London SW9 7AA.
Tel: 020 7450 0620; fax: 020 7450 0650;
e-mail: LMaudslay@skill.org.uk

Supported employment

Emma Krasinska   Manager, Hackney Recruitment Partnership, Unit D2,
3 Bradbury Street, Dalston, London N16 8JN.
Tel: 020 7241 5588; fax: 020 7249 3455

Leisure

Louise Jacklin   Policy Development Manager, Newham Leisure Services,
Town Hall, Barking Road, East Ham, London E6 2RP.
Tel: 020 8472 1430

Involving service users

Andrea Whittaker   9 Stanhope Avenue, London N3 3LX.
Tel/fax: 020 8346 7325

Policy and management issues/service re-design

Margaret Gregory   Service Manager, Knowsley Social Services,
Municipal Buildings, Cherryfield Drive, Kirkby,
Merseyside L32 1TX.
Tel: 0151 443 4197; fax: 0151 443 4210

Becky Loney   ISR Co-ordinator, Lifestyles Lewisham,
                    29–39 Clarendon Rise, London SE13 5ES.
                    Tel: 020 8852 9761; fax: 020 8297 2572

Barbara McIntosh   Community Care Development Centre,
                    157–168 Blackfriars Road, London SE1 8EZ.
                    Tel: 020 7928 7994; fax: 020 7928 4101

Les Truin   Manager, Horison NHS Trust, Harperbury Hospital,
                    Harper Lane, nr Shenley, Radlett, Herts. WD7 9HQ.
                    Tel: 01923 854 861; fax: 01923 855 909

Simon Whitehead   Acting Director, National Development Team,
                    St Peter's Court, 8 Trumpet Street,
                    Manchester M1 5LW.
                    Tel: 0161 228 7055

Care management

Angela Cole   Freelance Consultant, 40 King Street, Maldon, Essex
                    CM9 5DY. Tel: 016218 57819

Ann Lloyd   Commissioning Manager (temp.), Newham Social
                    Services, Broadway House, 322 High Street, London
                    E15 1AJ. Tel: 020 8519 5454; fax: 020 8557 8755

Maggie McMahon   Network Training. Tel: 020 8806 1502/020 8986 2046

Finance

Ann Lloyd   Commissioning Manager (temp.), Newham Social
                    Services, Broadway House, 322 High Street, London
                    E15 1AJ. Tel: 020 8519 5454; fax: 020 8557 8755

Easy-to-read summary

Introduction

This book has been put together in a way we hope will help anyone who wants to know what it says.

We hope that

- people with learning difficulties

- parents/families

- staff

- managers

will all be able to read it and find new ideas and good ways of working.

We hope the pictures and symbols will be helpful. Most are quite straightforward, but the ones below might need some explanation.

advocate

strengths

help/support

services

needs

together

person with complex disabilities

work/job

planning circle

Pictures and symbols taken from: *A Guide to Using Symbols*, Phoenix NHS Trust; *Rebus Glossary*; *Picture Communication Symbols*, Mayer-Johnson, People First publications, The Drawings Pack (NACVS, Sheffield).

Chapter 1

What the Government says about the lives of people with complex disabilities

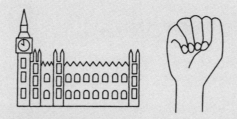

 A number of Government documents set out the rights of people with complex disabilities and how they should get the help they need to live a good quality life.

 People with learning disabilities – like everyone else – should live in and be part of their local community. This means having opportunities to:

 • go to college

● have a job

 ● have a home of their own

 ● get good health care.

 These opportunities should also be available to people with complex disabilities. The Government says that this should happen.

 However, many people with complex disabilities are still not getting opportunities for work, education, making friends and getting out and about in the community.

 Government departments in England, Scotland and Wales are working to try to make sure that people responsible for local services for disabled people take action to provide more opportunities for people with learning difficulties, including those who need a lot of extra help in their lives.

Chapter 2

Person-centred planning

Person-centred planning means supporting each person to make a plan of what they want to do in their life, the help they need to do it and who will help them.

It means working out specific goals or aims for the person.

- Some goals are easier to achieve quite quickly – for example to go swimming once a week

- Other goals are more difficult and take longer – for example, finding a different place to live

- Some goals might be big dreams — like getting on *Top of the Pops* or climbing the Himalayas!

The important thing is that the goals should be what the *person* wants — not just what other people think they need or want, or services say they can have.

The person should be allowed to have the fun of dreaming 'impossible' dreams. They might not get to sing on *Top of the Pops*, but they might be able to have a trip to London to see the programme being recorded.

Andrew Williams had a dream about climbing the Himalayas and did it! His circle of support helped him raise the money, plan the trip and train to get fit for climbing.

Planning circles

One of the best ways to make a lifeplan is to ask a group of people you know well to help you. This might be friends, family or staff.

The group meets regularly, perhaps at your home, or at a café or at a pub. You spend time talking about your lifeplan – but you also have fun – enjoy a meal, chat with your friends.

In Changing Days we called these groups planning circles. Sometimes they are called circles of support. Doris Clark has a circle of support in Bristol:

My circle is really good. At last I have people who will listen and understand. I have confidence now and go out such a lot.
My circle has helped me be the person I always knew I could be. (Circles Network Annual Report, 1997–98)

People with complex disabilities may need a lot of help to take part in their planning circle. It is important that everyone in the circle knows how the person communicates. Sharing information about the person helps everyone to get to know them better.

In Changing Days we worked with 45 people with complex disabilities in three different places – Newham, Knowsley and Harperbury Hospital. Each person had a planning circle to help them make a lifeplan.

Managers used the information from the lifeplans to see what changes were needed to make the services better.

PLANNING

Starting the planning circle

When a person decides they want a planning circle, they can choose to run it themselves or have someone to help them run it. If the circle is for a person with complex disabilities, they will almost certainly need someone to help. This person is often called a facilitator. It should be someone the person knows well. It might be a friend, a family member or a staff person.

The role of the facilitator

The facilitator's job is to:

- help the person set up the circle

- help the people in the circle work well together

- help the circle get things done to make the person's life better.

PLANNING

Person-centred planning days

These were days when up to five planning circles met together to learn how to make a lifeplan.

People said how much they enjoyed the informality and friendliness of these days and the feeling of everyone working together and helping each other.

Good things about this way of working

- The person with disabilities is the most important person in the planning circle

- Everyone tries to put the person's needs and wishes first

- Sharing information in the circle meetings helps everyone get to know the person better

- When there are difficult times, the people in the circle can help and encourage each other to stick with it!

- It is an enjoyable and fun way of doing things

The future

Because of the good things that happened for the people who were involved in Changing Days, the services are going to aim for every person to have a person-centred plan and a planning circle to help them.

This should mean that people's lives change for the better because they are getting what they really need and want.

> ### *Read more*
> You can read more about person-centred planning on pages 4–15.

Chapter 3

Communication

Being able to communicate our needs, wishes and hopes is very important for all of us.

If we can't let people know what we want – if we can't tell someone when we are in pain, or even when we are hungry or thirsty – life becomes very difficult.

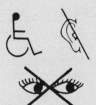

Many people with complex disabilities find it very difficult to tell others what they need and want. Many don't speak or use signs, and may even find pictures and photographs difficult to understand. They have to rely on other people to speak for them.

This chapter talks about ways of getting to know what someone with complex disabilities is trying to say to us. There are a number of stories about individual people – for example, Sara, a young woman who can't speak or do anything for herself. She needs help to get up in the morning, get dressed and even to move around in her wheelchair. She has to be helped to eat and drink without choking. Yet Sara enjoys life and even has a job.

You can also read about Vera, Mike and Roger.

Their stories teach us many important things about helping people with very complex disabilities to communicate and enjoy life. For example:

- each person must get good health care – like sight and hearing tests – in case this is what is making communication difficult

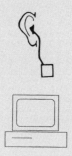

- each person should have any equipment or aids that would help them communicate, like hearing aids, electronic picture boards and computers

- each person should have any equipment or aids that would help them do more for themselves, like special switches on their wheelchairs to open doors or turn on the TV

- it is important for people to get special help with communication, like speech therapy and learning sign language.

We need to listen carefully and watch how someone is communicating. We must try to understand what their 'language' is – what they are trying to say in their own way. Then we can 'talk' to them in their way and learn more about how to improve their lives.

It is important to remember that this may take a very long time. Managers must give staff enough time to get to know individuals very well.

You can read about Sara, Vera, Mike and Roger on pages 16–35.

Read more

You can read more about communication on pages 16–35.

Chapter 4

Keeping fit and healthy

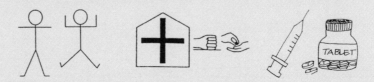

People with learning difficulties should get the same good quality health care as everyone else in the community. This means:

- going to a GP who knows the person well and who is helpful

- taking part in health screening programmes (e.g. blood tests, tests for allergies, tests for cancer)

- learning about healthy lifestyles (e.g. diet, exercise, sexual health).

People with complex disabilities often have a lot of extra problems with their health. If they are to have a good quality of life it is very important that they get good help from their GP and other doctors to keep fit and healthy.

People with complex disabilities often don't get good health care because:

- they don't see their GPs as often as other people with the same sort of health problems

- they sometimes find it harder to say how they feel or what's wrong with them

- they don't get enough health checks, such as blood pressure checks, sight and hearing tests, or advice on diets when they are overweight

- keyworkers and other staff often don't know enough about the symptoms or signs that someone might be ill

- sometimes parents and families also don't know enough about people's health needs.

What helps?

Each person's individual plan should include a section about their health, whether they take any medication and the support the person needs to keep fit and healthy.

The person's GP and other health staff should take time to learn how each person communicates – how they let others know when they feel sick or are in pain.

Every person should have a detailed health check with his or her GP once a year. This should be extra to ordinary visits to their GP.

What can services do?

A lot of people now agree that much more needs to be done about the health of people with learning difficulties. The Department of Health and big national organisations are working to make services better.

Keyworkers and other support staff should have training to learn more about the health needs of people with learning difficulties.

GPs need more training about how to help people with learning difficulties. They also need to work out how to give people more time when they come to their surgeries. Some GPs now make sure that people with learning difficulties get double the time at each visit that they give to their other patients.

Medical students should learn much more about people with learning difficulties during their training in medical school.

Read more

You can read more about health care in the community on pages 36–48.

19

Chapter 5

Education

 People with complex disabilities should have the opportunity for education just like other people with learning difficulties.

Because of their disabilities, they usually find it too difficult to learn in the same ways as non-disabled students do. So each person needs to have a programme of things to learn and that is made especially for them. It should be right for their age and level of ability.

It is important that people:

 • learn things that will be useful to them, like feeding themselves

● enjoy what they are doing

● have some success so that they will want to keep trying to do even better.

Some of the things people learn may seem very small and simple. But if you have many disabilities, a small skill can be a great achievement. For example:

● learning to use a switch to turn on a tape recorder

● being able to hold a spoon to help feed yourself

● being willing to take part in a group activity

● learning to make choices using objects – e.g. using a wooden spoon to choose cooking.

Being included with non-disabled college students

People with complex disabilities often need a lot of extra support to take part in college activities. This might mean:

- gradually getting used to being in a noisy, busy college

- finding your way around different buildings

- knowing how to buy a drink in the coffee shop.

Communication difficulties, personal care needs and unusual behaviour can make it difficult for people to be included in an ordinary college. However, as long as teachers and staff take time to get to know the person really well, he/she will learn new skills and enjoy being at college.

Read David and Bill's stories on page 56.

22

Read more

You can read more about education on pages 49–59.

Chapter 6

Transition

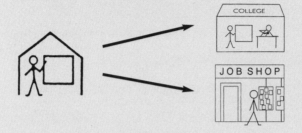

Transition means:

- getting ready to leave school

- thinking about what you want to do when you leave school – e.g. go to college, get a job

- planning how to make this happen.

It is one of the most important stages of a person's life – a time when many important decisions about the future are made.

It should be a time when opportunities open up for people, when they can make more choices and become more independent. However, for young people with complex disabilities, it can be a time

24

when they get less choice and not much help to plan what they want to do.

Transition planning

Government documents say that the young person's hopes and wishes should be at the centre of any decisions made about their future. However, there are a number of things that stop this happening for people with complex disabilities. For example:

- not enough time is spent listening to what the young person wants

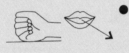

- there are not enough advocates who can help a young person say what they want

- it can take a number of visits to a college before a young person with complex disabilities can decide whether she/he would like to go there. Colleges often don't allow enough time for this to happen

- planning for the future is more than just deciding which college to go to. Young people with complex disabilities often don't get the chance to think about other things like where they want to live and who they want to live with, or what they want to do in their spare time. Also, they usually don't get the chance to 'dream' about the future like other young people do.

Helping parents

Transition can be a difficult time for parents. They know their son or daughter will still need a lot of support, but they also want to 'let go' so she/he can become an adult and be more independent. This is particularly hard for parents of young people with complex disabilities. Sometimes professionals seem to 'take over' and parents can feel shut out.

Parents and professionals need to work together to make sure transition is a good time for everyone.

People from different cultures

Ideas about growing up and becoming an adult can be very different in different cultures.

This means that making decisions at this time of life can be difficult for any young person who comes from a minority ethnic group. What they want to do might be very different from what their parents want them to do.

It is important to remember that this can be a problem for young people with complex disabilities as well.

What helps?

Managers in education, health, social services and the careers agency must work together to make transition a better time for young people. It will help if they:

- listen to what the young person wants and put his/her needs and wishes first in all decisions

- make time for professionals from the different services to meet together to discuss how to make transition easier for people

- sort out some of the present rules and regulations that make it more difficult for young people to get what they need and want

 !

- remember that young people with complex disabilities may take longer to decide what they want to do in their lives and, so, will need help and support for longer than other people.

Read more

You can read more about transition on pages 60–72.

Chapter 7

Supported employment – including everyone

 Having a job is very important to many men and women with learning difficulties.

 People with complex disabilities can also get jobs, if they are given the right training and support.

Finding out what a person wants to do

 If someone has very complex disabilities it can be difficult to know whether they would like a job or not. We need to think of different ways to understand what they want.

For example, a man with complex disabilities may not be able to say in words that he wants a job, or know what a job means. However, if he seems bored or frustrated or depressed, these might be clues that he wants something useful to do; that he wants to feel valued like other people. Finding him a job might be the answer.

Another way of learning what a person wants to do is to look at what they are good at and what they really enjoy doing. For example, if a woman with complex disabilities is always curious about new things and likes meeting new people, a job involving welcoming people might be a good idea.

Read Razia's story on pages 73–83, which describes how staff at the employment agency found Razia a job in an office and how it changed her life.

Often, people with complex disabilities do not get the chance to make important decisions about their lives. Other people always make decisions for them. Probably no one believes they could have a job so they don't know what jobs are available or how to choose one. So people with complex disabilities need to have the chance to try a lot of different things to see what they like and what they don't like.

Helping staff to work well

Staff in employment agencies have learned a lot about how to help people get jobs, including men and women with complex disabilities. But sometimes they run out of ideas or get stuck on a particular problem. It helps if people work as a team, sharing what they know about a particular person, sharing ideas, talking to other professionals and talking to the person's family.

Job coaches – the people who teach the person how to do the job – need the skills to teach people properly. One-to-one support is very important. The job coach needs to stay with the person and support them for as long as they need to learn the job well, to get to know their workmates and get used to the place where they are working.

Getting employers to help

Employers often want to give jobs to people with disabilities but are not sure how to do it.

Staff need to:

- go and talk to employers

- encourage them to offer a job to someone with complex disabilities

- explain how they will help employers support the person.

Staff need to talk to employers about the sorts of jobs that are available. Perhaps there are some jobs employers never get time to do. Perhaps there is a job where accuracy is more important than doing the job quickly. People with learning difficulties are very good at doing jobs accurately — that is, without any mistakes — even though sometimes they might take longer to get the job done.

Local authorities and health authorities can help by finding jobs for people with complex disabilities in their offices. Sometimes this can be done by looking at the work that needs to be done — like filing, photocopying, delivering mail round the building — and making a job specially for someone with disabilities.

Read Darwin's story on page 110.

A job can change your life

Razia's story shows how much a job can make life better for someone with complex disabilities.

This should happen for more people with complex disabilities so that they too can:

- become more confident and proud of themselves

- earn money of their own to spend

- become more accepted in their local community.

Read more

You can read more about supported employment on pages 73–83.

34

Chapter 8

Looking for leisure inclusion

Every person with learning difficulties, no matter how severe their disabilities, should have the chance to take part in local community activities. This includes having interesting things to do in their spare time.

Newham Leisure Services provides a lot of opportunities for leisure for people in the local community. For example:

 • leisure centres

 • parks and gardens

 • libraries

- sports grounds

- museums

- a farm and a nature reserve

- a zoo

- music and arts.

For disabled people, Newham has worked on improving physical access to buildings and providing 'special' programmes, like special times when people can use the swimming pool. Managers wanted to do more to include people with disabilities, particularly people with complex disabilities.

Four people with complex disabilities taking part in Changing Days wanted to do more at the leisure centres. This did not happen as fast as everyone would have liked but in the end some people did get what they wanted.

What helped?

A senior manager in Leisure Services and two staff took part in three people's planning circles. This meant that they got to know the person better and the sort of support she/he needed.

The senior manager really wanted to get things done and was able to get staff interested too. This meant that problems were solved more easily. For example:

At one of the swimming pools there was no suitable place for a very disabled young woman to get changed. It was arranged that, for the moment, she could use the First Aid room when she came for a swim. Plans were made to turn another room into a changing room, which any disabled person could use in future.

Other things that help

Find out whose job it is in Leisure Services to develop new opportunities for people. Invite them to get involved with people with complex disabilities.

Find out about all the leisure opportunities there are locally. Make up a book about places that are accessible and friendly to people with disabilities. User groups in Newham and Knowsley did this during their Changing Days work.

Offer to help train staff who work at leisure centres, libraries, sports grounds, etc. They need to know more about people with learning difficulties and how they can support them to use leisure facilities.

Read more

You can read more about leisure on pages 84–88.

Chapter 9

Creative movements in day services

This chapter is about a day service for people with complex disabilities who live in Lewisham. It is part of a day centre for people with learning difficulties.

The service supports eight people with complex disabilities. Eight full-time and three part-time staff work with these service users.

All the group use wheelchairs. They all have epilepsy. They need a lot of help with personal care, moving about and eating and drinking. The staff who support them need to know a lot about First Aid and other things like breathing problems and physiotherapy.

Each person has a weekly timetable of activities that they have chosen. Some of these take place in the centre, like music, relaxation and massage. But more and more time is spent out in the community using places that everyone else uses, like the bowling alley, snooker hall, leisure centres, college classes and art groups. The bowling alley has provided special equipment so that people with complex disabilities can take part, and has organised a competition.

Learning about each person

Keyworkers help service users build up a detailed picture of their lives – their likes and dislikes, their progress and achievements. This is done in several different ways:

- one person uses a laptop computer to record photos of his favourite pop stars, and photos and voices of his family. He can press a switch on the headrest of his wheelchair to trigger effects. Using the computer he can also tell people how he likes to be helped to eat and drink and how he communicates

40

- other people use photograph albums. Photos can be better than words to tell others about your needs, what you like and don't like, your dreams and favourite pastimes. One person has a photo of the hand movements he makes when he is upset and wants to be left alone. Other photos show how he likes to sit while eating and how he can be helped to hold his own spoon

- people also have folders and a locker where they can keep things like certificates of achievements, personal video recordings and audio cassettes.

Individual planning

Individual planning meetings are held every six months. Everyone who knows the person has a chance to contribute information in some way. Not everyone goes to the meeting: only people the person wants to be there. Keyworkers ask the service user and the parent or carer. Other family members and friends are welcome to come if it is what the service user wants. For example, one person's taxi driver who has become a good friend came to a recent meeting.

 Keyworkers often video someone's activities to show at the meeting. This can be a much better way of 'reporting' than writing or saying it in words and it is also relaxing and fun to watch. Recently, a service user won a prize in a London-wide bowling competition. This was a great achievement. Special equipment at the bowling alley meant she could bowl by herself, and she was able to show her winning moment to her parents on the video.

Keeping people safe

  Because every person in this group needs such a lot of support with their health needs, staff need to plan very carefully to make sure that they are not putting people in risky or dangerous situations. For example, if someone doesn't seem to be very well, it might not be a good idea for them to go out for their usual visit to the bowling

42

alley: they need to stay at the centre where they can get the special medical care they might need.

Because the staff really want the people they support to have the same opportunities as everyone else, they have become very good at working out ways for people to enjoy doing things out and about in the community, in spite of their very great health needs.

Community links

The group takes part in a weekly workshop for people with profound and multiple disabilities. They compose their own music, using computers and other aids like switches. For example, they are doing a project about transport and journeys. They record the sounds and voices they hear on their journey to the workshop and use the sounds to make music.

They have also joined with pupils from local schools to perform in two big concerts.

The school pupils now understand a lot more about disabled people's needs and everyone has enjoyed the experience.

The group also goes to a 'Getting to Know You' course at a further education college. This is a weekly class about personal skills. One week they may take photos of each other in fancy dress, and then create pictures by putting the photos together. The next week they might all meet up in a café and exchange news about their week. This has become a very popular class with both service users and staff.

The variety of interesting activities that this group take part in shows that it is possible to give people with complex disabilities the same sort of opportunities out in the community as other citizens have.

Read more
You can read more about day services on pages 89–100.

Chapter 10

Keeping users central – working together in groups

User involvement usually means people with learning difficulties working in groups to speak up for themselves and work with professionals to change services. This works well for most people with learning difficulties, including many who are physically disabled. Self-advocacy groups now do include people who use wheelchairs, for example, and provide support for people who can't see, hear or speak very well.

But being in groups does not always work well for the people this book is about – people with many disabilities who need a

45

great deal of support in their lives. Often they don't like being in groups at all. They are only happy with one or two people they know and trust.

Usually they don't use words to communicate. They need someone who knows them very well to help them 'speak up'. Even then, it can still be difficult to work out what they feel or want.

BUT ...

People with complex disabilities have a right to have their voices heard the same as anyone else. We must make sure this happens.

How we worked

The Changing Days project worked in three places – Harperbury Hospital (Hertfordshire), Newham (London) and Knowsley (Liverpool). A lot of other people with learning difficulties were involved also. People were speaking up for themselves in different ways in each of these places.

Speaking up as individuals in Harperbury Hospital

The people living in Harperbury Hospital had many disabilities, which would make it difficult for them to understand what a self-advocacy group was all about. Some people didn't like being in groups – they would only allow one or two people they knew really well to be near them. Others would need a lot of help over a long time to learn to speak up as a member of a group.

However, each person had their own way of communicating what they thought about their lives and what they liked and disliked. Most of them needed help from a member of staff or relative to do this. In Changing Days, they did this in their planning circles.

During the Changing Days project, some good things happened for most of the people involved. Managers and staff listened to what people wanted and their lives changed for the better. Now all the other residents in the hospital are being helped in the same way. So, although they didn't meet in a self-advocacy group, they have helped to change the way things happen in that service in the future.

 All the people involved in Changing Days were due to move out of hospital to new homes in the community. We had plans to try to link up with self-advocacy groups near their new homes. We thought the local group might, for example, like to befriend people from Harperbury. However, we didn't have enough time in the project to do this. Some people's plans changed or were delayed so we did not know where everyone was going or when. The people who did move out needed a long time to settle into their new homes and get to know new staff. The project finished before we could try out our ideas.

Speaking up in groups in Knowsley and Newham

In Newham and Knowsley, we also worked with a specially chosen group of people with complex disabilities. However, in these two places there were also many people with learning difficulties who were already speaking up for themselves and who were keen to be involved in the Changing Days work.

In Newham, there is a well-established People First branch office. A Changing Days user group was set up, with people from local user groups and day centre committees. It was organised and led by People First staff and very well supported by day centre staff and local managers.

Knowsley had once had a day centre self-advocacy group. A number of people who had been members of that group were keen to get it going again. They also had enthusiastic and helpful managers and staff to support them. So a Changing Days user group was quickly set up.

Aims of the user work

The two user groups decided on the following aims:

 ● show how staff and users can change services together

 ● help staff to listen

 ● make user groups stronger

 ● help people learn about new choices – e.g. college, office work, photography club

● help people understand how their lives might change.

  Thinking about people with complex disabilities in particular, they decided to:

- see how people who need a lot of support might be involved in checking services

- see how the user group might directly help people with complex disabilities – e.g. by getting involved with one or more planning circles

- make a book about places to go and things to do locally that are accessible and friendly to people with learning difficulties, including people who need a lot of support.

Successes

Having People First in Newham was very helpful. The Changing Days group could use their skills and experience in running groups and working with professionals. The group made a book of accessible places to go and things to do locally. Members also helped with a survey of what people in day centres thought about their services.

TAKING CONTROL

The Knowsley group needed to spend more time getting their group going again. They are now called the Taking Control group and have become the voice for people with learning difficulties in the area.

They organised their own user conferences and made a presentation to the Social Services Committee about what they wanted from day services.

They have also started collecting information for a book of local accessible places to go and things to do.

What helped?

Enthusiasm of service users.

People enjoyed working together and organising meetings and conferences. They learned new skills and became much more confident about speaking up for themselves and working with professionals to change services.

Support from managers

Managers came to meetings and conferences. They listened and took action to help the groups. They provided extra money for things like holding conferences and paying someone to make meeting notes easy to read.

Support from staff

Day centre staff and others who work with people every day helped the groups a lot. For example:

- getting to meetings

- learning how to organise and run meetings

- preparing to give speeches and presentations

- going out and collecting information about the local community.

What was difficult?

Not enough staff time.

Staff wanted to help more but couldn't because of other responsibilities in their jobs.

Staff changes

Some staff left or changed their jobs. It took time to find other support or for a new person to learn what was needed. This sometimes made it difficult for a group to get jobs done.

Involving people with complex disabilities

Both groups spent time talking about how they might get to know and work with some of the people with complex disabilities who were part of the Changing Days project. For example, there were plans to try to get involved with the planning circles. However, there was not enough time in the project to make this happen. By the end of the project, Knowsley group had decided to involve someone in their meetings and the Newham group had talked about how to arrange an outing for a member of the group who uses a wheelchair.

Both groups wanted to keep on working out how to make sure people with complex disabilities could have their voices heard and how their groups could help this to happen.

Conclusion

Involving people with complex disabilities in self-advocacy groups is a difficult job.

PLANNING

Perhaps the best way to make sure their voices are heard is to help them speak up, one by one as individuals, through their planning circles. In Changing Days, good things happened for people in this way and services began to change.

Rather than expecting people with complex disabilities to be involved in meetings, perhaps it is better for user groups to think how they could speak up on behalf of people with complex disabilities.

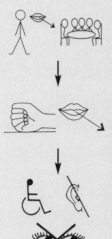

Perhaps some members could get to know a few people with complex disabilities, and find out what they want and need – what they like and don't like. They could bring information and ideas back to the group meeting and talk about what the group could do. For example, they might speak to managers about how the group thinks services should change to help people with complex disabilities.

It is important to make it possible for any person with disabilities to be involved in meetings and groups if that is what they want. But we also need to remember that being in a group may not be the best way for some people to get their wishes and needs known. We must keep working to make sure they are not forgotten.

Read more

You can read more about user involvement on pages 101–107.

Chapter 11

New lifestyles –
managing the changes

 Many managers want to make sure that people with complex disabilities have better lives. Changing services is a difficult job. Managers need a lot of skills, including:

- having good ideas about how to make services better

- being good at talking to people and making sure everyone knows what's going on

- helping other people to be leaders too, including users, parents and staff

- getting everyone to work together.

Getting agreement about a better future

Managers need to get everyone involved – staff, parents, carers, users – to agree about the sort of services they should be providing. Some of the important things to get people to agree about are:

- people with complex disabilities should have the same opportunities in life as anyone else

- this is more likely to happen if everyone in the different services – health, education, leisure, etc. – works together

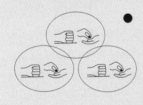

- every person should have a personal plan about their needs, hopes and wishes

- what people say in their personal plans should be used to make a plan about providing the best services

- services should not be in special buildings but should be alongside non-disabled citizens in leisure centres, colleges and local places in people's neighbourhoods.

Making big changes in services

Making big changes in services is a difficult job for managers. Sometimes they can get too involved in trying to work out new ways for making the organisation work better rather than getting on with the job of making people's lives better.

Managers can do a better job if they spend more time thinking about what is actually happening for people, and less time worrying about the organisation.

Understanding people as individuals

Everyone has a different personality. Everyone has different ways of communicating. Everyone has different needs and wants to do different things in their life. Services need to make sure that each person with complex disabilities can speak up for him/herself.

They need to make sure that parents and staff and anyone else who knows the person can share their knowledge of that person.

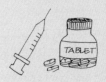

Each man or woman with complex disabilities should have a personal plan that includes things the person can do – not just things she/he can't do. It should say what the person does now – but also what she/he would like to do in the future. It should include important things like what medicines the person needs to take, but it should also include important things like helping the person make new friends and have a good social life.

Managers need to make sure that all the staff know how important the personal plan is, and to try to do what it says the person wants and needs.

Helping individuals get what they want and need

More people want to have a greater say on how money is spent. They want more control over their own money and more choice about who supports them in their life.

There are a number of things managers can do to help this happen, including:

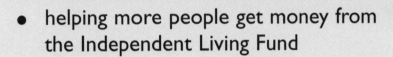

- helping more people get Direct Payments

- helping more people get money from the Independent Living Fund

- letting users choose who supports them

- always involving users in interviewing for new support staff

- supporting users and carers to evaluate services.

Changing the way staff work

In order to help people have the sort of lifestyle they want, staff will need to work in different ways. For example, staff will need to work at evenings and weekends, not just during the daytime, Monday to Friday.

There will be different jobs for staff to do. For example:

- job coaches – supporting people in real jobs – for example working in an office, or a café or a supermarket

- health support workers – helping people learn about how to keep fit and healthy and how to get on well with their GP

- community link workers – getting the local community to welcome people with disabilities into activities like clubs, neighbourhood groups, religious organisations, minority ethnic communities and all sorts of leisure activities.

Changing the way the community thinks

Managers need to work out ways of making sure that people with complex disabilities have opportunities in the community. It will help if:

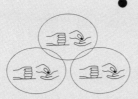

- senior managers in all the big departments work together. This means not only health and social services but also education, leisure and community organisations

- all big plans for a local area include the needs of disabled people – like making sure that all buildings are accessible and that staff in those buildings understand how to support people with complex disabilities properly

- local councillors want to make big changes for people with disabilities

- GPs and other health staff who work with GPs understand the sort of help that people with complex disabilities might need.

Making real changes in people's lives

Making big changes in services for people with complex disabilities is not an easy job for managers. But it must be done if people are to have better lives.

Read more

You can read more about managing service changes on pages 108–118.

Chapter 12

Thoughts from service managers

Two service managers – one from Knowsley and the other from Harperbury Hospital – wrote about what happened in their services during the Changing Days project.

Good things

- The lives of the people with complex disabilities changed for the better

- Staff learned a lot about how to help people with complex disabilities

- Staff got to know people and their families a lot better

65

- Managers learned some good ways to organise services differently and how to give staff better training

Things that were not so good

- There were no notes of what had happened to some people in the past. This made it difficult for staff to build up a picture of some people's lives to help their planning circle

- When people move out of hospital to a new home a long way away, it is difficult to keep track of how they are getting on in their new life

- It took a very long time for staff to find out what some people with complex disabilities wanted in their lives. Staff were worried about not having enough time for other people who needed their help

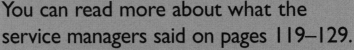

Read more

You can read more about what the service managers said on pages 119–129.

Chapter 13

Measuring progress

We wanted to see how people's lives changed during the Changing Days project.

At the beginning of the project we did a 'picture in words' about what each person's life was like. For example, what they did during the week, the people they knew, the skills they had.

At the end of the project we did another 'picture in words' to see how things had changed. For example, were they going out more in the community, did they have any new friends, had they learned to do more for themselves?

Some of the things that had changed were:

- most of the people were more confident and were 'speaking up' for themselves more

- five people had a job or were doing work experience

- some people were doing more things for themselves in their homes

- a lot of people were doing more things in the community. For example, one young man joined the Everton Football Supporters Club in Liverpool

- a few people had new friends.

Read more

You can read more about how people's lives changed on pages 130–135.

68

Chapter 14

Care management

Care managers help people with learning difficulties make their community care plan about what they want to do in their lives.

In their book *Oi! It's my assessment*, People First describes a care manager like this:

A care manager is the person that will work with you to try and make sure that you get the things you want and the support you need. This usually involves having an assessment. This is a meeting when you and people who know you will be asked lots of questions about what you are good at and what support you need.

What does the care manager do?

The job of a care manager is to:

- find out what the person with learning difficulties wants to do in his/her life and the support they will need to do this

- ask other people who know the person well how they think life could be better for that person

- draw up a plan for the person's life

- find the best possible people and places to provide the services the person needs to achieve what they want in their life

- arrange for the person to get those services.

This sounds like quite a straightforward, easy job for the care manager. But it is often made difficult because:

? • the care manager has to keep to a budget, so there might not be enough money for what the user wants

? • there might not be very many services for the person to choose from

• the services that are available might not be what the person wants.

Other things that can make it difficult are:

• there are not enough care managers to do the work

• they are not able to spend enough time getting to know users really well

- they have to spend too much time in meetings and doing paperwork when they would rather be talking to users.

What could help?

Planning circles could help care managers. The circles are there to help the person make a plan for their lives. They could pass on the information to the care manager.

This could help because:

- planning circles are made up of people who know the person well

- they can spend as much time as the person needs to get his/her wishes across

- in a planning circle, the person with learning difficulties can say what she/he *really* wants to do – not just what professionals think she/he ought to do. She/he can be allowed to dream and have wishes about the future.

Another idea would be for planning circles to have a budget. They could help the person decide how to spend the money. For example:

- to pay for someone to help them learn a job

- to help them get involved in the local football supporters club until they made friends there.

It would be important to work out clear rules and guidelines about how the circle managed a budget to make sure the money was kept safely and used in the right way.

Care managers have a very important job to do but they need more help to do it well. It could be *very* helpful to people with learning difficulties, including those with complex disabilities, if services talked more about how planning circles might help care managers.

Oi! It's my assessment. A guide to all you ever wanted to know about Community care, your assessment and your care manager. London: People First.

Read more

You can read more about the job of care managers on pages 136–141.

Chapter 15

Finance

 New-style day services mean that managers have to work out new ways of getting money and new ways of spending it.

 At present, a lot of the money for services is used up in buildings. But new services are much more about people than buildings. Also, service users go to a number of different places during the week – not just the day centre. This means that it is more complicated to organise and run the services. So the way the money is used will be more complicated.

If services do a really good job of person-centred planning and make sure that each person has an individual plan – and gets a service that is specially organised for them – it means that it will be more complicated to divide the money up to pay for people's services.

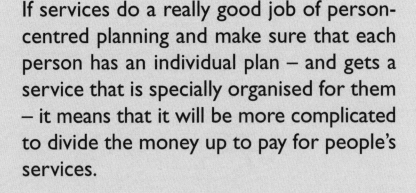

This is a very difficult task for managers and it is not easy to work out the best ways of solving the problems.

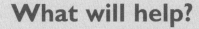

What will help?

- Managers finding more ways for people with learning difficulties to be able to buy their own services. There would need to be rules and guidelines for how people could do this and who could support them

- Managers finding different ways of using money – for example departments working together to share costs

- Managers finding different ways of getting more money – for example from local firms and businesses who might work in partnership to help people get jobs

- Planning circles may be a good way of helping with budgeting. Circles often cost more when they first get going, but over time they will probably save money, particularly staff wages. This is because they make better use of staff time and as people get more friends in their circle, staff can move on to help someone else

- It could help when people with learning difficulties, including people with complex disabilities, use more ordinary places in the community like leisure centres, colleges and community centres. These places have money to use for everyone in the community, including people with disabilities

Read more

You can read more about finance on pages 142–157.

Chapter 1

The policy context

Policy relating to services for people with learning disabilities whose needs are more complex is, in theory at least, no different to policy relating to all people with learning disabilities, and indeed to disadvantaged people generally. Whilst more specific guidance from the 1992 circulars[1] (on day services and health care) and, more recently, *Signposts for success*[2] (health care) is still in force, services for people with learning disabilities fall within the Government's more general initiatives relating to employment, education, health, social care and local government.

The buzzword of the moment – inclusion – has ironically been the mission of many of the more visionary services for people with learning disabilities for many years. Now it has been adopted by governments and influences many of the measures currently being put in place. Its adoption is welcome, for it embraces the notion supported by many self-advocates and 'champions' for some time – that people with learning disabilities, like everyone else, should have opportunities for inclusion in the mainstream of ordinary life. This means opportunities for life-long learning, for work, for support that promotes independence and for homes of their own, with access to both general and specialist health care according to individual need.

None of the new measures specifically exclude people with complex or multiple needs and, as stated, in theory there should be no reason why they should not have the same rights and access to opportunities as everyone else. In practice, however, we know that the impact of policy fails many people, particularly those with more complex needs. The Government's own commissioned research (see *Facing the facts*[3]) highlights how limited choice is for many people with learning disabilities, in terms of alternatives to traditional day care, whom they live with and where they live.

So although policy themes of welfare to work, promoting independence and life-long learning are to be applauded, it is uncertain how far-reaching these initiatives will be in terms of delivery. In particular, will people with more profound and complex needs experience any improvements in the opportunities offered to them? The answer to this question is more an issue of local implementation than policy and in terms of 'policy context' raises issues of the role of the centre in policy process – setting standards, performance monitoring, quality assurance, service and staff development guidance and initiatives, and of course resourcing.

Thankfully, this has been recognised. The English Department of Health has announced that it is to produce a strategy in the autumn of 2000, which will specifically address issues of equity, accessibility and what can be done to ensure that local services respond positively to policy guidance. Similar work on redefining policy and its implementation is under way in Scotland and Wales. It is the intention that all these initiatives will pay particular attention to the needs of people with profound, multiple or more complex disabilities. It is to be hoped that attention will be focused on the additional support that these people require so that they too can be included, and not on the making of exceptions of some people in some circumstances.

In the meantime, it is up to local services to work on how existing opportunities for supported living, employment and healthier lives can be provided for everyone – including those with more complex needs.

References

1. Department of Health. *Social care for adults with learning disabilities (mental handicap)*. LAC (92) 15. London: DoH, 1992.

Department of Health. *Health services for people with learning disabilities*. HSG (92) 42. London: DoH, 1992.

2. Department of Health. *Signposts for success in commissioning and providing health services for people with learning disabilities*. London: DoH, 1998.

3. Department of Health. *Facing the facts: services for people with learning disabilities: a policy impact study of social care and health services*. London: DoH, 1999.

Chapter 2

The person-centred planning process

Understanding someone's aspirations cannot be achieved by functional assessments or using checklists. It can only come about through sustained intense personal contact, friendship and understanding – and a willingness to make informed guesses, accepting that we still get it wrong at times. (Changing Days, 1996)

Developing a service to match the unique requirements of each person is ... the bedrock on which services should be built. We must transform a service which expects people to fit into a limited number of activities to one which evolves a range of choices from what individuals say they want to do or would like to try. (Days of Change, 1998)

Person-centred work challenges existing organisations, professional roles and personal lifestyles. It challenges workers to push back against the demands of the system to have the time, energy and heart available to respond to people. (Mount, 1990)

In the first phase of the Changing Days project, five development sites worked to put the needs of individuals first, striving to respond to the principles and values inherent in the above quotes. A number of different ways of developing profiles or assessments of people's needs and wishes were used, which influenced change in services to a greater or lesser degree. This process and its effect on services are recorded in detail in both *Changing Days* and *Days of Change*.

In the second phase of the project, we focused even more on person-centred planning (PCP) as central to the work, aiming to build on the 'best practice' experience of the first phase to learn more about effective ways of using a person-centred approach to achieve organisational change.

In each of the three second phase sites, we began by looking at the individual needs and wishes of a group of people and the support they would need to achieve their goals. We then used the aggregate of those needs to consider what this meant in terms of changes to day services.

This approach not only fulfilled the goal of rooting planning and development of services in the needs of individuals, it also helped to avoid becoming immersed in the labyrinthine complexity of attempting to change all aspects of a service at the same time – an approach that can too easily result in a focus on producing the perfect plan rather than achieving change in the lives of individuals. As *Days of Change* puts it, it is not about a clever piece of service design or redesign with definable inputs, clusters of need and blocks of service response. It is about a different starting point and finishing line:

This approach requires a radical change in the way we think about the job we have to do – a move away from 'developing services' and towards 'providing appropriate personal supports for individuals'.

Person-centred planning

The process we used is essentially an adaptation of personal futures planning[1] and Essential Lifestyle Planning,[2] plus ideas gained from experience of working with circles of support.[3] The essence of the process was to develop a planning circle around each of the 45 individuals selected by the three sites, and to actively involve everyone in the planning circle in drawing up for each person a lifeplan with specific short- and long-term goals and an action plan.

Appendix 2, the Personal Planning Book, developed during Changing Days has been adapted from materials produced by South & East Belfast Trust, Hackney Social Services and Ely Hospital during the first phase of Changing Days and by Newham NHS Trust in the second phase. Experience of the process of planning circles had also been gained during the work at Ely Hospital.

Michael

Michael is a man of 49 years who has had a severe disability all his life. He lives with his parents and uses the local day service. Michael uses a wheelchair. Since his circle started, an OT has been to his home to assess what adaptations would be helpful. The circle has also found a new form of community transport and through this he will, hopefully, be able to visit his sister's home.

Michael loves music. With help from his circle, he has renewed contact with a former music teacher who has sent a tape and a photograph. He has been to a concert at the Barbican Centre.

Michael has also renewed contact with an old friend he used to know at the day centre. His friend has visited Michael at home.

Michael's circle has extended to involve seven people, including his parents, his sister, his brother-in-law and three former day service staff. No one in Michael's circle is paid to be involved.

The facets of circles of support that proved valuable to us in the Changing Days work were:

- right from the start, getting together people who knew the person well to share their knowledge of that person

- involving friends, family and other 'unpaid' people
- using informal settings for meetings and working in informal ways
- focusing on talents and abilities
- including people's hopes and dreams for the future.

It is important to note two significant differences between circles of support and the planning circles developed in this work. Circles of support ideally operate outside of services and are made up mainly of unpaid citizens. However, many of the people we worked with, particularly people who were in long-stay hospitals, relied to a great extent on formal services and had no one in their lives except paid staff. Much preliminary work was necessary, to research people's family histories in the hope of perhaps reuniting with a family member or discovering a long-forgotten connection that might bring someone into the circle. So, while the planning circles formed through Changing Days phase 2 could not claim to be ideal circles of support, they know what they are aiming for and will gradually move towards that goal as people become more connected in their communities.

To follow our person-centred planning process, the essential steps are:

1. Select the service users who are to be the focus for the work
2. Agree who is to be the facilitator for each person's planning circle
3. Hold a training day for facilitators
4. Support the focus person, with help from their facilitator if necessary, to choose people to be members of his/her planning circle
5. Hold the first person-centred planning day with people's circles
6. Complete the person-centred plan, including agreed short- and long-term goals, when and how action is to be taken and who is to do it
7. Agree the date of the next planning circle meeting
8. Review achievements and redefine goals if necessary

The role of the facilitator

The circle facilitator's role is twofold; to help the focus person clarify their vision for the future and who they would like to help them with this; and once the circle has been formed, to keep it on track.

Facilitators ... keep members on task, record the main points in the meeting, and secure commitments to action from individual members. The facilitator also has to nurture the active participation of circle members, particularly those who may feel less confident about speaking or unsure of their contributions. Everyone can contribute something and the facilitator's role is to draw out people's gifts and value them.[3]

The basic tasks of the facilitator are to support the focus person to set up their planning circle, ensure it meets regularly and keeps focused on action and outcomes, and to help the circle members work together effectively.

Where the facilitator is a member of staff or a paid facilitator, she/he should work towards eventually handing over facilitation to an 'independent' or 'unpaid' member of the circle. This allows the original facilitator to move on to support other circles.

The following list sets out the facilitator's role in more detail:

- help the focus person identify who they want in their circle
- support the person to invite people to the person-centred planning day and subsequent circle meetings. Involve him/her as much as possible in preparing and sending the invitations
- ensure that the person with learning difficulties is at the centre of the process and that it is his/her views that shape all decisions
- maximise the person's participation in the meetings, e.g. using signs, symbols, photographs, video, etc.
- let the focus person increasingly take the lead in circle meetings
- facilitate the circle at the PCP day and subsequent meetings
- help the circle combine its skills, talents and knowledge to take an active part in extending the person's social network, opportunities and ordinary relationships. The facilitator should *not* have to do all the work
- help the circle identify what help and support the person may need to achieve his/her goals and agree the level of risk to be taken in achieving the goals
- keep the circle focused on action and positive outcomes for the individual
- keep everyone in the planning circle involved – encouraging them through the difficult times and celebrating successes – however small.

Choosing the facilitator

The facilitator should be chosen by the focus person – someone she/he trusts and relates to very well. The facilitator should be someone who can advocate for that person independently, without any conflict of interest.

But as the box setting out the role of the facilitator shows, this is a diverse role, which needs more skills than just being able to empathise with the focus person. The facilitator needs to be creative and generate new ideas; to have the confidence to lead and encourage a group; to be able to help the circle and the individual manage risk in order to take advantage of new opportunities; and to have the commitment and tenacity to persevere through tough times. Put like this it sounds like a lot of hard work, but circles are also about having fun – sharing food, making friends, enjoying socialising. If a circle does not seem to have anyone readily available to take on the facilitator's role it can be a good idea, provided the focus person agrees, to have two people sharing the role.

In the case of the planning circles at the three Changing Days sites, all the facilitators were members of staff. Often the facilitator was the person's keyworker or a care worker from where they lived. Obviously, this is not ideal for the reasons discussed elsewhere in this chapter, but is a likely starting point for many services aiming to put the person-centred planning process into practice.

Peter Hayward

Peter is registered blind. He enjoys walking and, through his circle, now goes walking in the park every other day rather than once a week. The circle contacted the Ramblers' Association and a volunteer has become Peter's friend. He now goes out once a month with ramblers.

Peter has moved to a new home and is getting more opportunities there. He has developed more independence – he does not always hold someone's hand or arm while walking and he has agreed to try using his white cane again. He often finds group activities like public sessions at the leisure centre too big and noisy but is learning to tolerate this.

The circle has begun to get more help with how to communicate with Peter and is getting to know more about his likes and dislikes.

Training for facilitators

Before the planning circles met for the first time, we held a training day for facilitators to explain the person-centred planning process and their role in it. This was an opportunity to make sure that people understood the principles and values on which the work is based and the ways of working that needed to underpin those principles and values, e.g.

- how to keep focused on positive aspects of the person's character, skills and potential
- the need to be creative
- strategies for keeping the circle going
- ideas for making community connections
- how to prepare for the PCP day.

It was also important that people had a chance to express doubts and fears, ask questions and share their expectations.

Supporting the facilitators

Support for people facilitating planning circles is crucial. Their role not only involves helping the individual achieve his/her goals and searching out new opportunities, but also keeping the circle working together effectively. This is a much more diverse role than is usually expected of day service staff. Some will take it on with enthusiasm and all that will be needed is support to allow their natural ability to blossom. Other people, embedded in the routine and predictability of the traditional day centre, find it extremely difficult to take on this facilitative role. The task is further complicated when facilitators have other duties within the service, which create conflicts of interest and pressures on their time and ability to make the sort of progress they would wish.

We found that one helpful solution was to have a member of staff with an overall responsibility to support the facilitators. This person's role was to meet regularly with the facilitators, be available to talk through difficult issues and to help with some of the problems and time-consuming effort sometimes associated with accessing a new community opportunity. Even more successful was the appointment of people with a specific remit to facilitate circles. They could work more 'independently' and concentrate on the development of the planning circles free of other responsibilities.

Person-centred planning days

To 'launch' the planning circles, we held person-centred planning days at each of the three sites, where several circles met to start putting together individuals' personal plans. We learned that the ideal number of circles to have at a planning day is five. A total of 25–30 people, which allows for an average of five members to each circle, seems about the right number to maintain informality and have time for everyone to get to know each other and share ideas and experiences.

We found that getting circles together at the beginning of the process was valuable for strengthening common understanding about the value and purpose of the work and for giving people a sense of ownership and of being part of a larger objective. Time and again, people said how much they enjoyed the informality and friendliness and the feeling of mutual support gained from the circles meeting together.

Sometimes the circles met for a full day, sometimes for half a day. With half-day meetings, two or three circles would meet in each half and everyone would join together over lunch. A full day gives more time for discussion about community building, including discovering more about the gifts, skills and community connections of everyone present, which might be shared among all the circles involved.

Practical tips for a successful PCP day

- Hold the day in a non-service venue if at all possible, e.g. a community centre
- Plan ahead! Give good notice in writing of the date, venue, etc.
- Family members may need extra support to be able to attend
- Invite a maximum of five planning circles to any one day
- Space needed – a room approximately 50' x 60' with good acoustics
- Make it as welcoming and informal as possible, e.g. colourful decorations, flowers, background music
- For each circle, provide chairs, a small table and a flipchart with paper and pens. Make sure the focus person sits near the flipchart. Circle members' attention tends to focus on the flipchart, so this helps to keep the focus person 'in view' and at the centre of things
- Agree ground rules at the beginning of the day, e.g. respect everyone's opinions – all ideas are okay
- Be specific when writing statements/goals
- Stay focused on the person
- Listen carefully
- Respect confidentiality
- Have an extra room available, equipped with a variety of things to do, for anyone who wants a break from being in their circle
- Have tea, coffee and soft drinks 'on tap' and provide lunch

Why did this approach to person-centred planning seem to work?

There seemed to be a number of factors that influenced the outcomes in this process:

- focusing on the individual as a person with gifts and abilities, rather than as someone with deficits and needs. Staying focused on positive outcomes for the person
- focusing strongly on relationships, social networks and community activities rather than services. This enabled 'person-centred' thinking rather than 'service' thinking
- informality and friendliness. Everyone in the circle seemed to put on their hat as an ordinary citizen rather than their professional or service provider hat
- it doesn't need a lot of paper work! All the essentials are there for getting to know the person and taking action towards achieving goals. The paperwork is fun and user-friendly – it is not a matter of filling in pages of detailed forms
- time. Staff valued the opportunity of spending more time than usual with people, getting to know them better as individuals and learning even more through the circle meetings. Making this time available was not easy for the services involved, but the positive results were seen to justify the investment
- parents appreciated the emphasis on their son or daughter as a person rather than a patient, and the fact that their knowledge was seen as vital to creating the person-centred plan.

This is not to say that concerns were swept under the carpet. Neither staff nor parents were afraid to be critical, and spoke frankly about fears and concerns. Understandably, some were sceptical about 'yet another meeting'! It was encouraging to see how people's views changed as they experienced the process. 'I had planned to go at lunchtime,' said one parent. 'But it was so interesting I stayed all day.' Another parent said: 'I've learned more about my son in the last two hours than I have in the last 27 years.'

Time and again, previously unknown facts about an individual were revealed through the sharing within the circle. Day centre staff learned to their amazement that a young man who never spoke at the centre did use a few words at home. In discussion, the circle realised that this was probably connected with the timing and effect of his medication, and so were able to consider possible changes to improve the situation. In another instance, a manager learned from the parents of a young man she had known for 12 years, that he used different coloured pens to indicate different wishes. Staff in another centre had always interpreted as 'please listen to me' a young man's gesture of putting his hand around his ear. On spending time with his parents, they learned that it was actually his way of asking for a pencil because his father is in the habit of keeping a pencil behind his ear!

Brett

Brett is a man with a visual impairment. Everyone in his circle has got to know Brett better and, though it's still difficult to figure out what really interests him, they are beginning to feel able to suggest more things he might like to do. The circle is trying to get help from a speech therapist to work out a way for Brett to say a definite 'yes' or 'no'. They are also building up a lifestory and communication book to help people get to know Brett more quickly. He has been out and about more than before – to Canary Wharf, the circus, a party at Leisure Link and the cinema.

Operational changes resulting from this method of person-centred planning

One way of judging the success of a particular way of working is the extent to which it is adopted over a whole service. In Harperbury Hospital, the process is to be used for every resident. To begin with, they will make sure that a lifestory book is put together for each person. A social inclusion section is being added to all care plans. A staff training pack based on the methods used in Changing Days is being developed for all the staff in the hospital.

In Knowsley, the process is being adopted by the whole service. Joint funding has been obtained to appoint a new member of staff to make sure that progress continues with the current work and to help set up new planning circles. Newham, too, is adopting the process over the whole service. They are appointing a new member of staff to have a joint role of co-ordinating the process and doing community building work, and will also be appointing facilitators to assist with the planning circles.

References

1. O'Brien J. A guide to personal futures panning. In: Bellamy TG, Wilcox B, editors. *A comprehensive guide to the activities catalogue. An alternative curriculum for youths and adults with severe disabilities.* Baltimore, MD: Paul H Brookes Publishing Co., 1987.

2. Smull M and Harrison SB. *Supporting people with severe reputations in the community.* Alexandria, VA: National Association of State Directors of Development Disabilities Inc., 1992.

3. Wertheimer A, editor. *Circles of support: building inclusive communities.* Bristol: Circles Network, 1995.

Further reading

Mount B. *Imperfect Change: Embracing the tensions of person-centred work.* Manchester: Communitas, 1990.

Chapter 3

Communication

Effortless, quick and accurate communication is one of the most complex and important skills of human beings. To be denied that skill severely limits our opportunities to make relationships, develop our personalities, and express our thoughts and fears. Many people with severe learning difficulties ... rely on interpretation by others of their unique methods of communication in order to be understood.

Those who work with adults with severe learning difficulties have always seen it as their role to promote effective communication skills, but many organisations don't give enough priority to providing the necessary training opportunities. The day-to-day relationship between the person who uses services and his or her support worker is of the utmost importance, yet it often seems that frontline staff are left without any real guidance. (Days of Change, 1998)

Being able to communicate our needs, wishes and hopes is a vital human necessity. This would seem to be a self-evident statement that needs no further discussion. However, experience during Changing Days made us realise how much more we need to learn about communicating effectively, particularly with people with complex disabilities (see Chapter 2, 'Person-centred planning').

This chapter illustrates two approaches to what it can mean in terms of skill, understanding and creative thinking to discover what someone with complex disabilities is trying to tell us. This is a crucially important starting point from which to develop services that effectively meet the needs and wishes of individuals.

Talking to each other

It is very difficult to get in touch with some people with severe learning disabilities. They do not respond to what we call current service provision; we are cut off from each other. We may be cared for, trained to behave acceptably in public places and live in comfortable houses but we cannot be part of a community if we are unable to communicate and interact. Communication is the precursor to social activity. It underpins confidence, equality, empowerment and friendship.

The first thing we need to look at is what we mean by communication. The following history relates a quite casual encounter at a day centre.

A stranger, I am invited to sit next to a shy, anxious young man at lunch. He keeps his head down and studies his hands, pushing his thumb along his fingers. Periodically he gets up and runs away. When he returns the third time, I put my hand on the table where he can see it – but not so close that it would seem threatening – and copy his movements. He notices at once and watches carefully, then looks up, smiles at me and takes my hand. During the afternoon, he repeatedly turns up at the open door of the room where I am working. Each time I spot him, I lift my hand, so he can see it, and make his movements. At the end of the day, he waits for me. I cross over the room, make his sign and say, 'Going home now?' He looks at me, beams radiantly and says, 'Yes.' I say, 'Goodbye' and we part.

This young man had learning difficulties, severe autistic spectrum disorder (ASD) and in practical terms was almost non-verbal. He rarely spoke and perceived people as difficult. He must have found being in a noisy building very hard and ran away from encounters or studied his hands – yet it was clear that he felt as good about our meeting as I did. We had given each other something that was precious. In a short time, he had developed the confidence to reach out and welcome a stranger.

This is communication at its deepest level. The technique used is called 'Intensive Interaction', which was developed by Nind and Hewett,[1] following on from work by Ephraim[2] and now used by myself[3] and many other practitioners, for example Ware.[4] Where people are locked into, or are predominantly absorbed by, repetitive behaviours, Intensive Interaction consists of observing those behaviours, recognising them as a non-verbal language the brain is using to talk to itself (a sort of personal code that is hard-wired in, non-threatening and safe) and reflecting them back, using that person's particular language as a framework with which to gain their attention. Through this, we can begin to build a conversation with them.

The ways in which a person can talk to himself or herself are infinitely variable. Here is a list of a few self-stimulatory behaviours that I have recently successfully worked through:

- using a person's sounds, including grunts and screams
- using a person's hand movements, finger and thumb rubbing or hand flapping
- working with rocking by:
  - tapping on their back in time to the rock
  - smacking the wall in time to their movement
  - smacking my leg in time to their movement
  - running a pencil up and down a corrugated tube in time
  - (working with a man who is blind/deaf) bouncing on the other end of the sofa in time to his movement
- sucking saliva
- echoing breathing rhythms
- banging feet.

In addition to internally generated behaviours using body parts, an individual may also hijack some object or theme from the world outside and use it as part of the furniture of their private language. In the following history, a woman crinkles a crisp bag as part of her way of 'talking' herself out of sensory stimulation she cannot cope with.

I am asked to find a way of working with Vera, who has severe learning disabilities with ASD. This is the first time we have met. She finds people difficult, particularly strangers, and has a number of ways of 'cutting out', including becoming totally absorbed in rustling and folding a crisp bag, examining its shiny surfaces.

I ask if I may sit next to her, pointing to myself and then the sofa beside her. She gives me a fractional nod of agreement. When I sit down she turns her back and starts to fold her crisp bag. Moving into her language, I also start to play with a crisp bag. She can hear its characteristic rustle although she is not looking at me. After a few minutes, she looks over her shoulder. We start a conversation with each other – she rattles hers and I follow. Suddenly she flings herself back across my lap and lies there, looking straight up at me and laughing as we talk to each other. This interaction goes on for about 20 minutes and ends when she loses my attention as I start talking to support staff about what we are doing. She sits up and turns away from me. I accept this, say 'Goodbye' and leave her.

Vera, who could not bear people, particularly strangers, was perfectly able to let me know that she enjoyed my company when I used 'her' language. It did not threaten her with sensory overload: she and I were able to share our pleasure in each other.

Details of working with people with a wide variety of repetitive behaviours may be found in *Person to Person*[3] and *You Don't Know What It's Like*.[5]

When we are 'talking' to someone, we give so many messages that are non-verbal. A feature of Intensive Interaction is that it follows the person's lead, giving them control so that they learn that what they do will have an effect on what others do.

There has always been the fear that working through a person's stereotypic and repetitive behaviours will reinforce these actions. In practice, I have yet to find a situation where this is so. On the contrary, it leads people out of the inner world they are locked into. Peeters[6] emphasises again and again that we must use the system that is most likely to succeed when communicating with an individual.

We must ask all the time: *is this way of getting in touch working for this person?*

People are sometimes worried that interactive techniques may not be seen as age appropriate. Perhaps the most telling comment on this subject came from a parent whose daughter, in her late 30s, had severe epilepsy, cerebral palsy and ASD. She was non-verbal and spent much of her time either in bed or crying. Three weeks after learning to use her sounds with her, her mother said, 'I used to have a child who I had to look after. Now I have a person I can chat to all the time.' This is a crucial switch from the role of carer to that of friend, from inequality to valuing – a quality we talk about a lot but, if we are honest, find it difficult to achieve.

Communication is a two-way process. Not only do we show the person that we are listening but, as we become more skilled, we can also learn to use their language in a variety of ways: we become more fluent in its use; we learn which elements indicate pleasure, what signifies security and when a person is becoming disturbed, and we can learn to transfer these with a positive emotional loading to situations where a person is unhappy. To use a computer analogy, we may describe the process as 'copy and paste'. This is illustrated in the following history:

Mike has learning difficulties and very severe autism. He spends much of his time outside in the garden. He finds people very difficult and chooses to separate himself from them. At intervals he presents himself at the door and says 'Drinks', with particular emphasis on the 'ks' at the end. It does not seem to mean anything to him to say 'soon' or some such time indicator. After he has had two, instead of replying, I try just repeating back to him his sound, 'ks', 'ks'. He is immediately interested and pays attention to me. We get a conversation going, alternating his sounds between us. He relaxes and stops asking for drinks. Instead of running away, he comes inside the house, we sit down on the sofa together and I whisper it in his ear and he likes it.

To understand this, we need to refer to Barron,[7] one of the authors of which is autistic. He tells us that in a kaleidoscope world of scrambled sensory information *when he used a repetitive behaviour he knew what he was doing*.

Mike knew what was happening when he was drinking. In between drinks, his anxiety rose. This could be allayed by tuning in to a contextual signal, one that he associated with drinks in a way that was also non-threatening. It was a sound that he could attend to without fear of fragmentation – of the signals from the outside world breaking up. Fascination with this new presentation of 'his sound' enabled him to be part of the world outside. His support staff use this as a way of making contact with him on a regular basis, both the sounds on their own and as 'bilingual' clues to draw attention to 'information', for example, 'ks, ks, Martin, Bath, ks, ks'. In this sense one is 'gift-wrapping' information in the language a person feels secure with.

Roger is also autistic with severe learning disabilities. He attends a large and, inevitably at times, noisy day centre – almost the last environment that one would think was a suitable background against which to effect improvement.

Roger wanders the day centre in a world of his own. He is disturbed by other service users and hits out at them if they come too near. He has quite frequent serious outbursts and is unable to take part in activities or even to go out on the centre bus.

Using Roger's sounds as an inner language to communicate with him resulted in a reduction in his 'difficult behaviour' and an improvement in his use of normal speech. He is now able to respond to other service users with a smile, go out in the bus with another person and, in the pub, put his money on the counter, say 'Coke' and wait for the change.

During this period of using 'inner language' to talk to Roger, staff focused not on teaching him how to do things but on how to be with him and communicate with him. Roger had always had a few words but has begun to use a wider range in an appropriate way. His latest achievement is to say 'Coke' to the barman, hand over his money and wait for his change. Each development – which may be a small advance to us – is a major step forward for him and enables him to move normally into a social situation that was previously closed to him.

At this stage it is crucial to emphasise that this work on improving communication with Mike and Roger, which was part of the Changing Days project, was not only dependent on finding new ways of communicating with them but also on integrating these within the structure of Essential Lifestyle Planning. Even when we know how to talk to people, it is only with management support, organisation and the dedication of staff teams that we can make effective change – particularly where inability to communicate is part and parcel of a whole range of disturbed behaviour. Structure and teamwork are vital. Without them, no amount of innovative input will have a lasting effect.

Managers' views

Listening to some of the managers of strategies that have had effective outcomes, the qualities they felt made for positive leadership were:

1. A management style that takes a pragmatic approach: 'If it works we will continue', 'if it fails we will reflect on why it is failing in a manner that is non-judgemental of staff'

2. Appointment of a change facilitator. This person is encouraged to come up with ideas and is supported by individual supervision

3. Staff need to be confident that, if they run into difficulties, leaders will support them with hands-on involvement

4. While a theoretical background is important, managers emphasise the value of practical objectives, such as 'what we are going to do this week?'

5. Keyworkers are encouraged to spread effective ideas laterally through their team to ensure consistency

Each step we take may seem a small one, but the effect can be cumulative and can transform the lives of people who are struggling to make sense of their environment.

Time

Time poses a lot of problems for people who do not understand intervals and sequence. Many people are worried about events like going home on the bus. Because they have difficulties understanding when an event will take place, they become progressively more upset as the time approaches for them to leave. They cannot match up their knowledge that the bus will come with the evidence that it is not yet here. They start to hit themselves and, in their confusion, when they do this they at least know what is happening. Using the technique of Intensive Interaction, I hit the wall with the same beat. They hear the rhythmic repetition of their self-injurious smacks coming from outside and are surprised, looking up for the source of the echo.

The loop of their inner turmoil is broken and attention is refocused, with the opportunity of re-establishing communication with the world outside.

In addition to dealing with the present crisis, we need to present time in a way the person will understand.

The answer is to make a clock *without the minute hand* (since this is visually confusing). The workings for an electric clock come in a small and cheap pack that is about the size of a cigarette packet and can be purchased from most watchmakers. The box has a spindle sticking out from the centre. All that is necessary is to drill a small hole, the same diameter as the spindle, through a piece of ply, push the spindle through and attach the hour hand only. Instead of numbers on the face, attach pictures round the edge using Velcro. In the instance that we are discussing, I would use one picture only, that of the bus, placed at the time it leaves. Because the hour hand is short, draw a line from the centre to the picture, so that they line up together at the correct time.

Now we have a visual aid to negotiation. Each time the question is asked, 'When's the bus coming?', we can redirect attention to the clock and answer, 'When the hand lines up with the picture.' The person who is anxious has something concrete to focus on and this can take the stress out of their situation. Gradually they may be able to cope with more than one picture and build towards understanding a day's activities. In order to give meaning to the idea of time we have to find ways of measuring and giving substance to it in a way the person can understand.

Self-injurious behaviour

Sometimes we can even work directly with self-injurious behaviour.

A woman is hitting her cheek so hard she has caused tissue damage as far as her cheekbone. Standing well away from her, I tap my cheek each time she hits hers. It is about 20 minutes before she notices what I am doing. Gradually I move closer, and eventually am near enough to gently tap her uninjured cheek each time she hits herself – an action that has become more gentle since she has noticed what I am doing. She starts to smile and then to test me, bringing in all sorts of movements of her hands and arms that were not part of her previous repertoire. She laughs each time I get them right.

Her keyworker continues to use this technique with her. After six weeks, of her own accord, she starts to bring a cushion and sit by the keyworker in the evenings, instead of running away. Although she still touches her cheek she no longer hits herself and is much happier.

Previously unable to bear physical contact, she will now sometimes collapse laughing into her keyworker's arms.

Living an ordinary life

When invited to join with a person with complex needs to help design his/her future, it is important to remain focused on positive outcomes that reflect ordinary life, rather than concentrating on 'fixing' deficits. Too often, the person's life rotates around an intervention rather than the intervention being integrated into and supporting their daily life.

Some guiding principles

- The ability to move one's body is essential to maintaining good health
- The ability to communicate, maintain good body position and eat food in the normal way contributes to a person's sense of well-being, health and interactive life in the community. Communication, body alignment and mobility are improved through the continued use of adapted or custom-designed aids and equipment, and the use of modern technologies

- Using tubes to help with eating may not have to be a long-term commitment. Supporters should continue to pursue ways that would allow the person to eat normally

Start by asking some basic questions ...

Question	Why is this important?
How well is the person positioned so that she/he can see and interact with people?	• People needing help to correct or control neuro-motor components of physical conditions may require adapted equipment and/or technological aid to facilitate proper seating and alignment. This can enhance learning, improve eye contact, independence, health and community integration • Correcting body alignment for conditions such as kyphosis, scoliosis and rotational deformities of the spine is essential to other activities • Correct positioning can prevent deformity and skin breakdown, and promote movement, e.g. conditions that affect the arms and legs, such as scapular contractures of the shoulder • Individuals whose lung capacity or heart function may be limited by poor posture must be properly positioned
How well does she/he control his/her environment?	Enabling control over as much as possible is essential. Adapted equipment, computer technology, trained animals, etc., have created a world often limited only by our imagination. From adapted toilet seats, beds, power chairs and eating utensils to sound/touch activated doors, lights, radios and TVs ... control at work and home is high on the agenda when enabling an ordinary life.

Question	Why is this important?
How does she/he receive information from others?	The extent to which the person can receive and act on information is also important in helping them to control their environment. People with sensory disabilities may need aids such as canes, tactile direction indicators, auditory cueing devices, safety alarms, adapted computers, guide dogs, hearing aids, visually enhanced safety devices, amplifiers, TDD, voice speak, etc.
How well can others understand him/her?	Relationships depend on the exchange of information. Individuals needing help to communicate and be understood may require: • speech therapy, manual sign language, language development • communication devices (augmentative or alternative), such as picture boards, speech synthesisers • supports such as switches, head pointers, press pads, mouth tubes, etc. • support staff who understand the person's use of gestures, sounds, expressions or language. New people providing support should receive training so that continuity in understanding how the person communicates is maintained.
Are mealtimes safe and enjoyable for the person?	Mealtimes should be a time of comfort, pleasure and social interaction. People need to be in the best position to eat food safely and normally. Therapeutic positioning during and after meals is mandatory. Appropriate ways to help the person, for example, learn to move his/her tongue to swallow, increase jaw movement, lip closure or learn to eat using a fork should be taught to anyone involved in mealtime assistance.

Question	Why is this important?
Is she/he well? Well-being looks at emotional, physical, spiritual and intellectual concerns.	Good health contributes significantly to the person's overall well-being. Emotional health fluctuations often depend on our relationships with others. Our self-concept is built on 'messages' about how others see us and is based on shared experiences. Positive, reciprocal interactions build confidence and self-esteem.
Being safe from harm is also a factor.	Good health comes, in part, from effective prevention strategies and awareness of how an overall healthy lifestyle contributes to 'wellness'. Access to knowledgeable and proactive health care services is critical.

A spiritual dimension to life brings, for many, peace, focus and a sense of 'oneness' or security. Relating with others who share the same belief system can contribute to a person's quality of life.

Experiencing and learning new things can bring joy, variety and excitement to our lives. Exploration and adventure adds variety and opportunity to life.

Being safe from abuse, neglect and damage from bad or uninformed practice is mandatory. |

Meet Sara ...

Sara was placed in a long-stay hospital at age ten because 'she was too big for her family to handle'. Now, age 29, she lives with two other women in her own home.

Sara's story is written in the first person, as if she was speaking to the reader. This imagined monologue is about a real person, although a pseudonym is used.

I turn and notice that hints of yellow and orange are beginning to dance into my room to announce the beginning of another day. I've been waiting for these familiar sun fairies with their sparkling dresses reflecting early morning colour. More of them will be coming now that they have found a window with curtains wide open in welcome.

I like early mornings. I like to lie here with the warmth of my waterbed wrapped around me. These very early hours set the tone of my entire day. These are the hours when I am free to think and laugh at thoughts others cannot hear. Sometimes I invite the water to act as my dance partner and we sway in unison to music I've turned on by touching the big button switch pinned to my bed.

I've heard people speculate about my 'biological clock' and how my biorhythms (whatever those are) must be better in the mornings. All I know is I don't want people to bother me until I'm ready. When I am interrupted too early I show my lack of enthusiasm by being grumpy and out of sorts for the rest of the day. It took an awful lot of very, very grumpy days before they finally learned to leave me alone until I was ready.

One of the other loves of my life – now – is food. I say now, because there was time when I was terrified of eating or drinking. Once I heard someone say I wasn't eating because of a 'failure to thrive'. Let's get this straight, I wasn't eating because of my 'demand to survive'. Every time someone came at me with food, I thought they were going to kill me. Finally, someone got a clue and started paying attention to where food was going when I swallowed it. Answer – my nose, sinuses and lungs.

Thankfully, the people who help me eat now pay a great deal of attention to how my head, mouth, throat and bottom are lined up when I eat. They also offer me food much more slowly and, I am very happy to say, they make sure the variety and consistency of the food I'm offered suits me.

Today, I greatly enjoy meal times. I'm always in the kitchen during meal preparation so that staff can talk to me about what they are doing. They let me check out each ingredient, savour the smells and anticipate the taste. It's like eating twice, once with my mind and again with my mouth. Not only that, but now I help train new staff in safe mealtime practices. How many people can say they get paid to eat?

Well, I guess it's about time to get up and get going. I'll make the sound that gets turned into an automated voice that says, 'I'm ready to get up'. Sandra and I are going to try out different computer programs today. I like bright colours and have been designing covers of greeting cards. Another friend of mine puts words inside some of the cards. Friends suggested we might try selling them at boot sales or markets. Why not? I enjoy being around people and activity – not to mention that I could use the money!

As I lie here and think about it, my life has changed a lot.

Mostly that's because of who came into my life. Most of the people in my life these days are people who have stopped working *on me* and are working *for me*. They don't see me as an object that needs 'fixing' but as a person with strengths and needs. I haven't changed as much as how they see me has changed. I am no longer transparent.

What Sara's file said ...

- Non-verbal, severe muscular contractions in all extremities
- Medically fragile, requires total care
- Tendency for hypothermia and skin breakdown/bed sores
- Disruptive sleep pattern
- Self-stimulation, rocking behaviour
- Challenging behaviours, e.g. whining, screaming in the mornings
- Aspiration, failure to thrive
- Has feeding tube
- Chronic phenomena and sinus infections

What happened ...

- Sara was connected to people who were interested and who cared about her. Some also had the knowledge, skills and interests she needed
- She now has support staff who work for her and explore with enthusiasm
- A lot of time was spent observing and listening to her and talking with those who know her best to understand her likes, dislikes, abilities, interests and needs
- New equipment enabled her to be mobile and positioned properly at all times
- She received an individually tailored communication device
- After a swallowing study, Sara's feeding tube was removed. She practised how to move her tongue to assist with swallowing, increase jaw movement and lip closure
- An individually tailored diet was developed for Sara, with food consistency based on preferences, skills and needs
- Access to a consultation team was provided, which included physio, occupational and speech therapists, dieticians and medical staff who worked with her at times and places that suited her daily routine
- Career and community opportunities were explored. New staff were trained
- She is active on advisory boards

Sara's life is in progress. It is difficult to know with certainty what her future will look like or what she and other men and women in similar circumstances will teach us about how to best support their efforts towards a fulfilling life (as defined by them). But as stories about people with complex needs living in the community are shared, we seem to be learning that they, with all their complex challenges, are very much like us. If my eyes age, I adapt and start wearing glasses. If I lose an arm in an accident, with a lot of support and adaptations, I try to get to the place where I can live the kind of life I want to live. If I lose my ability to speak or hear or see, with the support of family, friends, technology, heath care and financing, I adjust and find my way back to ordinary life.

Conclusion

It is through sharing experiences that we make friends, have allies. We become more prepared to engage with the world outside. This is empowerment. Communication is vital: it is not just about the exchange of information but also about building relationships and letting each other know we feel good about each other. This builds confidence. It is confidence rather than conformity that changes the way that people with learning disability are viewed by, and integrated into, the community.

The moving-on picture – multimedia profiling

The advent of computers, and information technology generally, has provided a valuable tool to help people with complex disabilities communicate. Multimedia profiling enables people with high support needs and very little verbal communication to tell others about themselves and their lives, and to take part in planning their future.

Acting Up worked for six months with staff, service users and carers in the three Changing Days sites to explore the possibilities of developing multimedia profiling. The work included information and training and the production of a profile of one person in each site. The service users involved were seen as having severe communication difficulties that to a great extent prevented their involvement in the life-planning process. The focus would be on their individual needs and supporting increased participation in education, leisure and work.

All three sites had some IT resources and computer-skilled staff and they were already using photographs to enrich text-based life plans. The training and production period explored a number of the stages involved in developing multimedia profiling, including video documenting, computer editing and presentation. The equipment used was a camcorder and laptop computer. Training took place in each site and at Acting Up's London base.

The final reports were drawn from the multimedia catalogues of video, sound and photo files created for each individual. They show aspects of each person's life – activities, places, people and events (past and present) – and present a comprehensive and positive picture of the service user's personality, needs and potential. Each profile will be used to maintain and improve the user's quality of life, and to empower them through such use.

Albert's profile

The profiling team reviewed video from a number of sources. They presented the first report to Albert's family, who took more video at home to add to his catalogue. The final report shows a wide-ranging programme of centre-based and other activities. Video clips of hydrotherapy sessions showed Albert's commitment to maintaining his physical strength and mobility. His patience and perseverance are clearly demonstrated while taking part in craft and cookery, and his awareness and communication skills are shown throughout the report.

Three key support workers spent a day at Acting Up being trained on the technical aspects of profiling, such as extracting clips from video taken at the sites, updating catalogues and making reports. They also discussed related issues, such as positive images, confidentiality and consent, and user-involvement.

There was commitment and enthusiasm for the work in all three sites. Participants were pleased with the outcomes and excited by the possibilities for the people profiled and for other service users. A number of benefits and uses of this type of profiling were identified:

- empowering users by enabling them to play a part in making and presenting information about themselves
- helping to get to know the person, e.g. new friends or new workers in 'handover' situations
- showing in detail the various ways a person communicates
- demonstrating needs and strengths in reviews
- identifying and agreeing goals and action plans
- providing clear illustrations of positive changes achieved and action needed.

Acting Up is part of the Matchbox Theatre Trust, which has since 1986 been working with people who are marginalised by severe communication difficulties and institutional attitudes. Their aim is to demonstrate that people with learning difficulties have a lot to say about their lives. By using information from the past and present in the form of still and moving images and with the help of a touch screen, people with high support needs and very little verbal communication can own this material, share it and help plan their future.

For more information on Acting Up, see p.72 of *Days of Change*.

Contact: Acting Up, 90 de Beauvoir Road, London N1 4EN. Tel: 020 7275 9173

References

1. Nind M and Hewett D. *Access to Communication*. London: David Fulton Press, 1994.
2. Ephraim GW. *A Brief Introduction to Augmented Mothering*. Radlett, Herts: Playtrack Pamphlet, Harperbury Hospital, 1986.
3. Caldwell PA with Stevens P. *Person to Person*. Brighton: Pavilion Publishing, 1998.
4. Ware J. *Educating Children with Profound and Multiple Learning Difficulties*. London: David Fulton Press, 1997.
5. Caldwell PA with Hoghton M. *You Don't Know What It's Like*. Brighton: Pavilion Publishing, 2000.
6. Peeters T. *Autism. From Theoretical Understanding to Educational Intervention*. Whurr Press, 1997.
7. Barron J and Barron S. *There's a Boy in Here*. London: Simon and Schuster, 1992.

Further reading

Conville RL and Rogers LE, editors. *The Meaning of 'Relationship' in Interpersonal Communication.* Westport, CT: Praeger, 1998.

O'Brien J and O'Brien CL. *Unfolding Capacity: People with Disabilities and Their Allies Building Better Communities Together.* Lithonia, Georgia: Responsive Systems, 1994.

Smull M and Harrison SB. *Supporting people with severe reputations in the community.* Alexandria, VA: National Association of State Directors of Development Disabilities Inc., 1992.

Rucker L and Ogle P. *Real Life, Real People, Real Choice: Community Plan for West Tennessee.* Herington, KS: Rucker, Powell & Associates Ltd, 1997.

Rucker L and Powell D. *My Choice? Ordinary Life: Community Plan for the State of Tennessee.* Herington, KS: Rucker, Powell & Associates Ltd, 1998.

With thanks to Pavilion Publishing for permission to use material from *Person to Person* and *You Don't Know What It's Like*.

Chapter 4

Health care in the community

Men and women with learning difficulties should benefit from all actions taken to improve the health of the whole population. They should have access to all health services, including health promotion and health education, programmes of health surveillance and maintenance, and primary and secondary health care, with appropriate additional support as required to meet individual need. (Days of Change, 1998)

Putting health care into context

One of the most important aspects of providing support for people with learning disabilities, along with maintaining independence and close contact with relatives, is making sure that they have access to services that meet all their health needs. For people with learning difficulties who have complex disabilities, health is perhaps the most crucial aspect of their lives to be addressed. Most of the people who were involved in the Changing Days project had a range of specific health needs and some relied on regular health interventions simply to stay alive.

The importance of understanding what life can be like for an individual in need of intensive health care support and some ways of making sure that person enjoys a more ordinary lifestyle is highlighted in Chapter 3. This chapter goes on to consider what that means in terms of delivering a high quality service that will cater for individual needs in as non-restrictive and non-medical way as possible.

Medical care for anyone with a disability has two roles – firstly, to preserve longevity and a good quality of life and, secondly, to facilitate social inclusion. Good medical care is about maximising the capacity to enjoy life to the full.

The role of primary care is to provide a comprehensive 'non-specialist' medical service near to where people live. Its importance within the national health system was recently emphasised in the White Paper *The New NHS: Modern, Dependable*.[1] As the doctor responsible for supervising health care in the community, the GP is an important member of the multidisciplinary team responsible for each person's life.

A large part of general practice involves responding appropriately to newly developed symptoms. Another less well appreciated but essential component is prevention – proactive investigation to prevent serious diseases, for example immunisation programmes, cervical screening and health education.

Health issues for people with learning difficulties

The majority of people with learning difficulties have always lived in the community, where they form 2 per cent of the population.[2] Not only do they develop the same illnesses as everyone else, they have much higher prevalence rates of long-term medical disorders – both physical and psychiatric (see Box 1). Also, their medical care can be made more difficult, to the point of a significantly increased risk to their lives, if they are unable to describe their symptoms or co-operate over examination, investigations or treatment. Further, as knowledge increases and treatment of illnesses becomes more complex, and as people live longer, maintaining people's optimum health will become ever more complicated.

Box 1: Comparison of disease prevalence rates		
	People with learning disabilities	General population
Epilepsy	33 per cent	0.75 per cent
Mental disorder (10 per cent having psychosis)[3]	50 per cent	25 per cent
Obesity[4]	19 per cent (male) 35 per cent (female)	6 per cent (male) 8 per cent (female)

Despite their relatively higher rates of mental and physical needs, and even though they make contact with GPs more than any other professional, most people with learning difficulties see their GPs less often than other groups of patients with a similarly large number of medical needs, for example elderly people.[5, 6] In recent decades a relatively small number of people with learning difficulties, some with multiple and complex medical problems, have moved from large institutions to homes in the community, and these people have been shown to generate a disproportionately increased workload for GPs.[7]

In 1986, Dr Gwyn Howells, a GP in Swansea, published the first of many research investigations that demonstrated how inadequately the health problems of people with learning difficulties are dealt with.[8] In 1993, Horizon NHS Trust completed an audit of primary medical care for people with moderate or severe learning disabilities living in Harrow.[9] The findings were measured against a standard set by the Royal College of General Practitioners, which recommended a comprehensive annual medical examination.[10] Only one of 42 people examined was found to be completely physically well. Three-quarters of them had at least one unrecognised or unmanaged medical condition, while a third had more than one (see Box 2).

Box 2: Number of unrecognised or unmanaged medical conditions in those examined

Previously unmanaged or unrecognised medical conditions	Number of patients	Percentage of those examined
1	18	43
2	6	14
3	5	12
4	2	5

Importantly, eight of the 12 patients found to have life-threatening, unmanaged disorders had been seen by their GP three or more times in the last year. This was consistent with the theory that regular annual medical examinations would identify unrecognised disorders, where opportunistic assessments during unplanned surgery visits clearly do not. Only 12 people (25 per cent) were known to have ever been offered a full examination by their GP (never mind examinations every year). Six patients (14 per cent) had significant physical signs obliging prompt medical attention, including heart murmurs, severe raised blood pressure and poorly-controlled diabetes. Half of all those examined were overweight to the extent of being at increased risk of suffering a heart attack.[11]

The most common physical problems were 22 people (52 per cent) with significant earwax – 15 affected in both ears – and 21 people (50 per cent) being overweight. Eleven people were considered to be obese and only two of these were on a diet.

Regular medical examinations

Some causes of learning disability are associated with an increased prevalence rate of specific illnesses, such as hypothyroidism (underactive thyroid) in people with Down's syndrome. These higher prevalence rates make it worth screening for illnesses that occur more frequently in people with specific syndromes. Thus, a regular blood test to detect hypothyroidism before it causes symptoms will help prevent complications such as coronary heart disease (see Box 3).

Box 3: Conditions associated with different syndromes causing learning disability

Syndromes	Symptoms/conditions associated
Prader-Willi syndrome	Short-sightedness Diabetes Hypogonadism (reduced oestrogen and testosterone secretion) Delayed puberty, obesity Osteoporosis Sleep apnoea
Down's syndrome	Visual and hearing impairment Hypothyroidism Alzheimer's dementia Congenital heart defects Sleep apnoea
Tuberous sclerosis	Retinal tumours Cerebral tumours Kidney and lung hamartomas
Neurofibromatosis	Endocrine abnormalities Tumours susceptible to malignant change
Cerebral palsy	Constipation Oesophagitis Anaemia
Fragile X syndrome	Mitral valve prolapse

It is important that the annual medical examination recommended by a number of authoritative organisations (see Box 4) is recognised as a form of screening, so as to contextualise it properly within the health strategy of the nation. Some organisations prefer the vaguer title 'health checks' but, although a number of the disorders identified might be causing symptoms already, they would have remained unrecognised and therefore untreated had the examination not taken place – thus remaining true to the ethical principles justifying screening (see Box 5).

Box 4: Organisations recommending annual medical examinations

---

Organisations and date of recommendation

Horizon NHS Trust (1970)
Royal College of General Practitioners (1990)
Welsh Health Planning Forum (1992)
Mental Health Foundation (1996)
Mencap (1996)
Department of Health (1998)

Box 5: Principles justifying screening

---

1. But for the investigation, an illness would have remained undiagnosed
2. The investigation is reliable
3. The investigation is not disproportionately invasive or expensive
4. Any illness diagnosed can be effectively treated

The role of carers in health care

Many carers of people with learning difficulties have only a limited understanding of their client's or relative's medical needs and have never been trained to recognise physical or mental illnesses, or to provide what sometimes amounts to nursing care.[12] They cannot be effective advocates until they are empowered with the necessary medical knowledge to enable them to negotiate a health system that can sometimes seem intimidating and obstructive, to the point of hindering proper access to both primary and secondary medical care.[13] Some GPs rely on carers to take responsibility for anticipating and identifying illnesses (see Box 6) when the most appropriate person for that role within the multidisciplinary care network may be the doctors themselves.[14]

Box 6: Symptoms of diseases associated with learning disability syndromes

Sleep apnoea	Snoring Restless sleep Abnormal daytime sleepiness
Diabetes	Drinking excessive fluids and passing excessive volumes of urine Weight loss Lassitude Drowsiness
Hypothyroidism	Lassitude Weight gain Hair loss Coarse skin Hypothermia Constipation Confusion
Oesophagitis	Poor appetite Vomiting Weight loss Evidence of pain related to mealtimes and lying down Difficulty swallowing food

Several recent studies have shown an increased prevalence of osteoporosis in people with learning difficulties.[15, 16] The Osteoporosis Awareness Day held at Horizon Trust in 1998 is an example of the way in which people with learning difficulties and carers can be armed with the knowledge necessary to act as skilled advocates in health matters. Educational material in the form of written notes, talks, short films, samples of food and demonstrations (including a fun run) was presented to clients and staff in an eye-catching way that stimulated attention and interest.

Screening programmes

There has also been concern that people with learning difficulties are not taking part in routine community screening programmes. One community trust found that only 25 per cent of eligible women with learning difficulties were undergoing cervical screening, compared to 82 per cent of the rest of the population.[17] In 1997 Horizon Trust, Hertfordshire Health Promotion and the Women's Nationwide Cancer Control Campaign co-operated over an intensive programme to screen the learning disability hospital's 128 eligible women. As previous experience had demonstrated the importance of securing carers' enthusiastic support, both staff and some patients participated in educational sessions. The Trust sex education team provided advice and educational models, and made themselves available in case the process provoked disturbing memories. As this was a screening and not a curative procedure, residents who refused consent were not tested and, although it was a routine public health measure, relatives were informed as a matter of good practice unless the patient specifically requested otherwise.

Of the 128 eligible women, 45 (35 per cent) took part in the screening. The remaining 83 (65 per cent) did not take part for various reasons, including being unable to participate because of physical or behavioural difficulties or refusing consent. The difficulties encountered due to the high number of people at Horizon with psychiatric/challenging behaviour/ physical disability when compared to people living in the community were to some extent offset by the logistically easier task of arranging the resource-intensive programme within a relatively small organisation.

Valuable lessons were learned from this programme – both about the importance of building in education, awareness and understanding of carers and residents in the preparatory stages and about the most effective ways to organise and carry out the screening.

Box 7: Possible causes of the increased prevalence of osteoporosis in people with learning difficulties

As a group, people with learning disabilities have an increased risk of osteoporosis over the general population. This is a result of:

- increased prevalence of low weight[a,b]
- fewer opportunities to exercise
- less interest in/appreciation of sport
- suffering from some specific syndromes that promote osteoporosis, e.g. Prader-Willi syndrome, Down's syndrome[c]
- decreased exposure to sunlight
- reduced intake of dietary vitamin D
- increased requirement for drugs that promote osteoporosis, e.g.
  - anti-psychotics that suppress oestrogen/testosterone levels
  - some anti-convulsants stimulate the breakdown of vitamin D
- people not being autonomous, and so being unable to take decisions to maintain their own health
- people having a degree of physical disability that:
  - leaves them reliant on others for exercise
  - decreases their capacity for exercise
  - means staff tend to use aids (e.g. wheelchairs) or transport to facilitate mobility.[d, e]

Notes

a) Simila S, Niskanen P. Underweight and overweight cases among mentally retarded. *Journal of Mental Deficiency Research* 1991; 35: 160–64.
b) The nutritional intake of people with learning disabilities. *Journal of the Association of Practitioners in Learning Disability* 1998; 15 (1).
c) Sepulveda D *et al.* Low spinal and pelvic bone mineral density among individuals with Down's syndrome. *American Journal on Mental retardation* 1995; 100: 109–14.
d) Lee J *et al.* Disorders of bone metabolism in severely handicapped children and young adults. *Clinical Orthopaedics* 1989; 245: 297–302.
e) Lin P, Henderson R. Bone mineralisation in the affected extremity of children with spastic hemiplegia. *Development and Medicine and Child Neurology* 1996; 38: 782–2.

The future

There is currently a surge of interest in establishing how best to deliver physical health care to people with learning difficulties. The Department of Health and influential national organisations are campaigning for improved standards. Many local authorities are developing new services to ensure that the health care needs of people with learning difficulties are met, such as appointing dedicated health liaison nurses to facilitate access to primary and secondary health care.

Despite the broad consensus supporting annual medical examinations, there is no consensus about what model of screening is best or about who should do it. Many models exist, such as nurse-led, GP-led or specialist doctor-led screening, but success tends to depend on the enthusiasm and diligence with which the service is provided rather than on the type of practitioner. Until research establishes what the health gain from regular screening is and which model is best, it is unlikely that any method will be adopted universally, with the risk that the quality of screening will remain inconsistent and the essential monitoring of standards will be plagued by difficulties resulting from comparing one system to another.

The medical care of people with learning disabilities living in the community, with its complex mix of family, social and medical problems, has always seemed a natural general practice responsibility. However, the burden of health care responsibilities within primary care has greatly increased in recent years and general practitioners are under great pressure, with a number of competing demands on their time and expertise. They have not only expressed concern about screening in general but also resistance to providing health promotion and regular health checks in people with learning difficulties.[18, 19] Nonetheless, some general practitioners have adapted their practice to meet the needs of their patients with learning difficulties by, for instance, doubling consultation times. Others resist assuming new commitments in this field.

Because of the relatively small number of people with learning disabilities, few general practitioners have the opportunity to develop much experience of their medical care. Fifty per cent of a group of general practitioners surveyed in one study said they lacked confidence in supervising their medical care.[20]

Two initiatives would improve health care delivery for this medically vulnerable group of people: firstly, more widespread adoption of the teaching of medical students about learning disabilities along the lines of the curriculum at St George's Hospital Medical School, where the subject is embedded throughout the undergraduate programme; secondly, the creation of a new post of community specialist in the physical health care of people with learning disabilities, which would be analogous with the national system of consultant psychiatrists in learning disabilities.[21, 22] The specialist could be responsible for raising standards of primary and secondary health care for people with learning disabilities through the education of health professionals, carers and clients; carrying out research; and personally supervising the health care for that group of people with complex health problems that generic health services have difficulty treating.

References

1. Department of Health. *The New NHS: Modern, Dependable*. London: HMSO, 1997.

2. Office of Population Census and Surveys. *The General Household Survey: Informal Carers*. London: HMSO, 1988.

3. Mansell J. *Services for people with learning disabilities, challenging behaviour or mental health needs*. London: Project group report, 1993.

4. Bell A, Bhaler M. Prevalence of activity and obesity in Down's syndrome and other mentally handicapped adults living in the community. *Journal of Intellectual Disability Research* 1992; 36: 359–64.

5. Evans G, Todd S, Beyer S, Felce D, Perry J. Assessing the impact of all the All-Wales Mental Handicap Strategy: A survey of four districts. *Journal of Intellectual Disability Research* 1994; 38: 109–33.

6. Singh P. *Prescription for change*. London: Mencap, 1997.

7. Chambers R, Milsom G, Evans N, Lucking A, Campbell I. The Primary care workload and prescribing costs associated with patients discharged from long-stay care to the community. *British Journal of Learning Disabilities* 1998; 26(1): 9–12.

8. Howells G. Are the medical needs of mentally handicapped adults being met? *Journal of the Royal College of General Practitioners* 1986; 36: 449–53.

9. Hall P, Regan A, Young J. *Audit of primary medical care of people with learning disability living in Harrow.* Horizon NHS Trust, 1993 (unpublished).

10. Royal College of General Practitioners working party. *Primary care for people with a mental handicap*. Occasional Paper 47. London: RCGP, 1990.

11. Seidell J. Effects of obesity. *Medicine* 1998; 26(11): 4–8.

12. Meehan S, Moore G, Barr O. Specialist services for people with learning disabilities. *Nursing Times* 1995; 91(13): 33–35.

13. Smith B, Win W, Cumella S. Training staff caring for people with learning disability. *British Journal of Learning Disabilities* 1996; 24: 20–25.

14. Howells G. Situations vacant: doctors required to provide care for people with learning disability. *British Journal of General Practice* 1996; 46: 59–60.

15. Centre J, Beagu H, McElduff A. People with mental retardation have an increased prevalence of osteoporosis: a population study. *American Journal of Mental Retardation* 1998; 103(1): 19–28.

16. Wageman A *et al*. Osteoporosis and intellectual disability: is there any relation? *Journal of Intellectual Disability Research* 1998; 42(5): 370–74.

17. Pearson V, Davis C, Ruoff C, Dyer J. One quarter of women with learning disability in Exeter have cervical screening. *BMJ* 1988; 316: 1979.

18. Mant D. Health checks – time to check out? Editorial, *British Journal of General Practice* 1994; 44: 51–52.

19. Kerr M, Dunstan F, Thepar A. Attitudes of general practitioners to caring for people with learning disability. *British Journal of General Practice* 1996; 46: 92–94.

20. Plant M. The provision of primary medical care for adults with learning disabilities. *The British Journal of Development Disabilities* 1997; 43(1): 75–78.

21. Cumella S, Corbett J, Clarke D, Smith B. Primary Health Care for People with a Learning Disability. *Mental Handicap* December 1992; 20: 123–25.

22. Beange H, Bauman A. Health care for the developmentally disabled. Is it necessary? In: Fraser W, editor. *Key issues in Mental Retardation*. London: Routledge, 1989.

Further reading

Keywood K, Fovargue S, Flynn M. *Best practice? Health care decision-making by, with and for adults with learning disabilities.* Manchester: National Development Team, 1999.

Langham J, Russell O, Whitfield M. *Community Care and the General Practitioner: Primary Health Care for People with a learning disability.* Bristol: Norah Fry Research Centre, 1993.

Welsh Health Planning Forum. *Protocol for investment in health gain – mental handicap (learning disabilities).* Cardiff: National Health Service Directorate, 1992.

Wilson D, Haire A. Health screening for people with mental handicap living in the community. *BMJ* 1990; 301: 1379–80.

Chapter 5

Education

Educational opportunities should be an integral part of the individual planning process and should have a clear purpose, whether related to employment, leisure or personal development.

Colleges and adult education should be seen as part of community provision, offering structured and individually tailored educational and training opportunities with appropriate support. The emphasis should be on progression: that is, devising a planned route through from one stage to another, with in-built preparation and transition arrangements. (Changing Days, 1996)

Education for students with complex needs can take many forms and take place in different settings. It requires an individual, needs-led approach, which demands flexibility, creativity and clarity of purpose. A key element is providing the means to enable students to progress towards achieving developmental goals. The challenges for providers and funding agencies are to adapt provision to suit the individual, rather than expecting the individual to 'fit in' with existing structures, and to ensure funding arrangements that will allow this to happen. This chapter describes the work of Orchard Hill College of Further Education, which aims to put these principles into practice.

Key elements of a curriculum for people with complex needs

Clarity and flexibility

A curriculum framework that is clear but flexible, and which can respond to the needs of each student, is required. The focus of each curriculum area should be relevant to the students and presented in ways that suit their age and level of ability.

Orchard Hill College has a broad-based curriculum designed for students with complex needs.

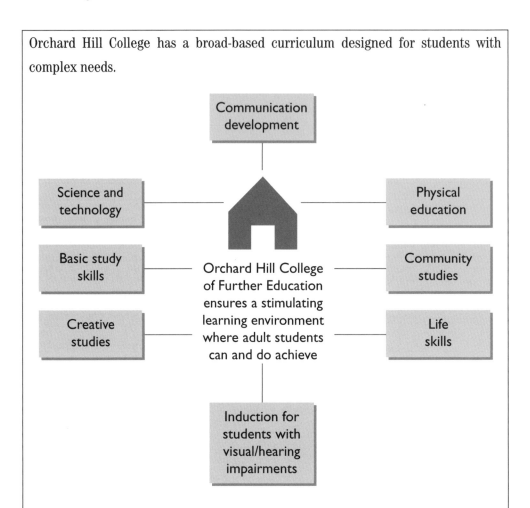

Additional study courses are attached to each core area so that students can opt for a more specific focus, e.g. swimming comes under physical education.

The Orchard Hill College curriculum will be available from David Fulton Press in 2001.

Enabling progress

The delivery of this type of curriculum requires skilled and creative staff and sufficient levels of staffing to enable each student to make progress. On average, Orchard Hill College students work in groups of six, with three staff per group. Some students need one-to-one support and the ratio may be increased at times according to need.

Specific objectives should be set for each individual, in consultation with the student and people close to him/her. Setting these objectives is important for monitoring and providing evidence of progress. Consultation with the student is often complicated by communication difficulties. However, there is evidence to suggest that close observation and recording of student responses can provide reliable indications of their views.[1]

Motivation

Motivation is the key to achieving individual goals. Learning can be achieved in many different ways and it is the responsibility of staff to discover individual preferences and approaches that suit the student.

Incorporating student views

Student choice and student evaluation should also be key components of the curriculum. Evaluation is best carried out during, or immediately following, a task. It may take the form of recording a student's non-verbal responses, such as pushing away/smiling, or recording a sign, word or vocalisation.

Choice-making should be integral to the entire curriculum. Some students need to be taught what making a choice means, understanding the different choices available and how to communicate their choice.

Sharon has profound learning difficulties and visual and hearing impairments. She communicates by gesture and sound. She loves foot massage. Objects of reference were used consistently to denote massage (a mat and a bottle), cooking (a wooden spoon) and other tasks. Sharon now makes choices using these objects. She usually chooses the mat and bottle, then stands up, feels her way to the mats, sits down, takes off her shoes and grins!

Recognition of achievement

Recognising achievement is critical for developing an individual's confidence, particularly for those who have often experienced 'failure' due to inadequate provision and lack of support. Recognition can become a part of each day through the development of an organisational culture that makes commonplace the celebration of every achievement, large or small. Awards ceremonies and certificates or records of achievement, in accessible formats, may also be used to raise awareness and recognition of progress.

Examples of goals for which awards are given

- Increased confidence in the use of an adapted switch to operate a tape recorder
- Willingness to participate in a range of tactile and sensory experiences
- Developing the confidence to interact with a new person in an unfamiliar environment
- Enthusiasm and participation in a group media project
- Consistently giving eye contact to objects and people when working with them

---

Formal accreditation is now available for students with complex needs (ASDAN, ALL, Open College). However, it is important that accreditation should not limit but enhance and enrich the curriculum and support each person's progress towards their individual goals. The following example shows how Orchard Hill matches the needs of the individual to the needs of the accreditation objective.

Life skills curriculum component	Identified individual need	ASDAN Independent Living module objective
Food preparation	To make choices about food and drink	Choose what you would like to drink

Inclusion – bridging the gap

Once again, the key to successful inclusion is to 'find out how each individual learns best'.[2]

People with complex needs often require specific support in order to make progress in inclusive settings. This may mean a carefully thought-out, gradual introduction to new environments and people (e.g. finding the way around a noisy, busy college building) or an induction course for learning or re-learning practical skills needed in the new setting (e.g. buying a drink in the coffee shop). Support may be short-term or may need to be on-going.

Communication difficulties, physical needs and challenging behaviour often prevent inclusion becoming a positive experience for students. Specialist teachers, or others with relevant expertise, can bridge the gap between specialist and integrated provision. Information, support and training for everyone involved are critical.

Staff from a specialist college accompany a small group of students with complex needs to a local school and work with the school-teacher in the classroom. One of the group, Paul, enjoys being with other people, but finds it difficult to communicate. Paul has a school 'buddy', Chris, who works alongside him and has learned to communicate with him.

Staff training and development

Staff working with students with complex disabilities need skills in many areas. For example:

- observation skills
- structuring creative approaches to learning
- dealing with challenges
- alternative communication systems

- providing personal care
- facilitating student choice-making.

To develop a quality service, managers need to create a plan of training and structured support for all staff. The plan should incorporate the needs of individual staff and the needs of the organisation as a whole. Most plans include an induction, training in new areas, refreshers and regular individual support sessions.

However, limited funds present a challenge for most managers. Training often includes two types of expense – direct costs like fees and travel, and indirect costs such as replacing staff during the training. Costs may be minimised by adopting some of the following tactics:

- identifying a time when all staff are available for training together
- establishing a system of feedback for passing on individual training to colleagues
- investing in training individuals in key areas so that the organisation has its own trainer/adviser in-house for different aspects of the work
- linking the staff development plan and budget to organisation development priorities
- ensuring that hands-on staff are given high priority for training (they are closest to the 'customer' and, therefore, affect quality)
- using support or 'mentor' meetings to resolve specific training issues
- using team teaching for 'on the job' training and skills sharing
- visiting places of good practice, which can be cost-effective by ensuring that the visit includes practical 'hands-on' involvement that enables staff to try new ideas and share them with colleagues on their return.

- The RNIB offers a Diploma/Certificate in Multiple Disability through a network of trainers in the UK and some overseas areas (Tel: 0121 643 9912)
- Practical, sometimes inexpensive, workshops are available from a range of providers. They are advertised in newsletters (e.g. *Focus, Information Exchange, PMLD Link*) and journals

Accessing funding

Potential sources of funds for educational provision for people with complex needs include:

- local education authorities
- the Further Education Funding Council/Learning & Skills Council
- social services
- charitable trusts
- health authorities
- NHS trusts
- European funding.

Managers often experience funding problems in relation to education for people with complex needs, depending on the type of their organisation and sometimes on the level of ability of the students. For example:

- small organisations can have difficulty in covering their costs if the funding agency's formula assumes that some costs, such as overheads, are already funded
- some funding agencies also create criteria for funding, such as prescribed timescales and outcome targets, which do not recognise the educational achievements of this group of learners.

Tapping into several different sources of funding can increase resources and raise awareness of the potential of learners with complex needs. However, managers are faced with the challenge of finding time to complete bids, juggle the demands of many sets of criteria and liaise with colleagues regarding multi-partner bids, in addition to carrying out other important aspects of their work.

Many people in the field have been attempting to raise awareness of the specific funding issues for students with complex needs. At the time of writing, a new White Paper *Learning to Succeed* had just been published. This has the potential for creating far-reaching changes in the planning and funding of educational opportunities for people with complex needs.

Positive collaboration

Collaboration between a specialist and mainstream service can facilitate access for students with complex needs.

> David attends the local college once a week. He uses a wheelchair and communicates using gestures and facial expressions. He finds busy environments daunting. He has attended a course at a specialist college for two years – part of a four-year course. In the first year, he spent most of his time in a specialist environment. In the second and third years of the course, his specialist teachers team-teach with the sector college staff to enable David and five other students to attend a course in the mainstream college.

Collaboration with colleagues in the field and with people in the community offers many benefits for students, staff and carers. It offers the chance to learn from people with different perspectives. For example, linking with other people who work directly with an individual enables sharing of information and techniques that work well for him/her in one setting but that may be unknown in another. These contacts, such as between education and careers services, can pave the way for further opportunities for students with complex needs.

> Bill attended a vocational skills course at a specialist college. He showed a clear preference for gardening placements, e.g. at the local ecology centre and a local park. At the end of the course, Bill moved on to Pathway Careers Service and now works one day a week with a job coach.

Collaboration checklist

- Gather information about potential partners
- Establish a relationship of mutual interest and respect
- Communicate clearly and frequently, avoid jargon
- Agree and clarify aims and actions
- Evaluate and share success

Conclusion

The experience of Orchard Hill clearly demonstrates that it is possible for adults with complex disabilities to take part in and benefit from educational opportunities. Commitment and determination to take action is needed from commissioners and providers of services to ensure that this group of people get the same opportunities as their more able peers.

References

1. Hogg J. Competence and Quality in the Lives of People with Profound and Multiple Learning Disabilities: Some Recent Research. *Tizard Learning Disability Review* 1998; 3(1).
2. Tomlinson J. The Findings and Recommendations of the Further Education Funding Council Learning Difficulties and/or Disabilities Committee's Report: Inclusive Learning. *Skill Journal* 1997; 57.

Further reading

DFEE. *Learning to Succeed: A new framework for post-16 learning.* London: DFEE, 1999.

FEU. *Learning For Life*. FEU Mencap, 1992.

Griffiths M. *Transition to Adulthood for Young People with Severe Learning Difficulties.* London: David Fulton Press, 1994.

Hutchinson M. *Discovery, Exploration and Problem-Solving for people with profound and multiple learning difficulties.* Winslow Press, forthcoming.

Lacey P. and Ouvry C. *People with Profound and Multiple Learning Disabilities: A Collaborative Approach to Meeting Complex Needs*. London: David Fulton Press, 1998.

SKILL. *Financial Assistance for Students with Disabilities in Further Education & Training.* London: SKILL, 1999.

Contacts

ASDAN Educational Ltd, 27 Redland Hill, Redland, Bristol BS6 6UX. Tel: 0117 923 9843; fax: 0117 946 7774; e-mail: asdan@uwe.ac.uk

Oxford, Cambridge & RSA Examinations, Coventry Office, Westwood Way, Coventry CV4 8JQ. Tel: 0120 347 0033; fax: 024 76 421 944; e-mail: cib@ocr.org.uk

Focus Newsletter, Multiple Disability Information Officer, RNIB (Royal National Institute for the Blind), 224 Great Portland Street, London W1N 6AA. Tel: 020 7388 1266; fax: 020 7388 2034; e-mail: glevy@rnib.org.uk

Information Exchange, 'Kenwoods', 53 The Circuit, Cheadle Hulme, Cheadle, Cheshire SK8 7LF. Tel: 0161 486 6514

Orchard Hill College of Further Education, 6 Elm Avenue, Orchard Hill, Fountain Drive, Carshalton, Surrey SM5 4NR. Tel: 020 8770 8125; fax: 020 8642 3763

PMLD Link, c/o The Editor, The Old Rectory, Hope Mansell, Ross-on-Wye, Herefordshire HR9 5TL. Tel: 01989 750382; e-mail: PMLD@mansell. wyenet.co.uk

SKILL (National Bureau for Students with Disabilities), Chapter House, 18–20 Crucifix Lane, London, SE1 3JW. Tel: 020 4750 0620; freephone information service: 0800 328 5050; fax: 020 7450 0650. e-mail: info@skill.org.uk

Chapter 6

Transition – moving towards adulthood

Transition is about change and 'new beginnings'. It should induce anticipation and excitement but also a healthy dose of anxiety because it is a venture into the unknown.

Service transition can cover moves to further education, vocational and residential placements. It is not only a time of change for the young person but also for their family.

Social workers, care managers and other professionals must ensure that both assessment and planning are organised effectively. Good advance planning gives everyone the chance to be prepared and promotes confidence in the process.

The young person ... should be at the centre of the planning process and actively involved in all decisions. Meetings to plan transition should not be held without them. All information available to the professional participants should also be given in a comprehensible form to the young people. (Days of Change, 1998)

The transition from being a young person at school to becoming an adult is one of the most important stages of a person's life. It should be a period of life when opportunities open up as a young person moves towards greater independence and self-determination. However, for young people with complex needs, it often becomes a time when options close down and choice becomes restricted.

This chapter begins with a brief overview of the current policy and legal context of transition for young people with complex needs. It then looks at a range of issues that are central to successful transition and at the problems that occur if they are not addressed. It ends with examples of good practice in transition.

The legal context

The Parliamentary Act dealing with transition is the Disabled Persons (Services, Consultation and Representation) Act 1986. This Act applies to England, Wales and, with some modifications, Scotland. It gives a young person who has a statement of special educational needs the right to a future needs assessment on reaching the age of 14. The 1986 Act is strengthened by the Transition Section of the Department for Education's *Code of Practice on the Identification and Assessment of Special Educational Needs* 1994, which advises on how this assessment should be carried out.

Local education authorities (LEAs) have to organise an assessment by including a transitional review as part of the first annual review that a young person has after their 14th birthday. The following people should be invited:

- the young person
- their parents or carers
- relevant members of staff from their school
- a representative from social services
- a careers officer.

Other relevant people can also be invited. The aim of the review is to draw up a transitional plan that should then be reviewed every year until the young person leaves school. The Code of Practice strongly emphasises that the young person's views must be central to both the review and the plan.

However, although certain local authorities have made a real effort to make transition reviews a success, it is apparent that in many cases the process is more of a token gesture than real. People who are meant to attend the review do not always attend and all too often school curriculum issues dominate the 14+ review, with only a passing reference to transition planning at the end.

Transition planning – some key issues

The place of the young person in decision-making

The Code of Practice explicitly states that the young person's hopes and aspirations for the future should be central to any decision made. In reality, however, many factors prevent this from happening for people with complex needs:

- often not enough time is given to actually listening to the young person, or enough effort made to support them with an advocate who could help them articulate their wishes

- young people with complex learning difficulties inevitably have problems conceptualising different options and will need to make frequent visits to potential future placements before they can begin to make a decision. Although some institutions do allow for this in the form of taster days or link courses, there is currently no clearly marked source of funding for this transition provision

- it is often assumed that transition for young people with complex needs is just about them making decisions about their future placement. But transition to adulthood is an holistic process, which also includes a young person's social and emotional development. Young non-disabled people explore these aspects of growing up through constant informal discussion with their peer group, away from parents and professionals, but this is all too often not an option for young people with complex needs

- young non-disabled people often make decisions about their future life by going through a period of fantasy. Although only a minute proportion of those who dream about being a rock star or football player actually achieve their ambition, this fantasy forms a necessary part of their transition to adulthood. All too often young people with complex needs are discouraged from such fantasies by constant reminders of the need to be 'realistic'.

The place of parents

The period when young people move from dependence towards independence can be a difficult one for parents, who have to try to find a balance between support and letting go. Letting go can be particularly hard for parents of young people with complex needs. They can be justifiably concerned about the isolation or discrimination that their son or daughter might face when they leave school. Parents' confusion over their role can be exacerbated when, in an attempt to stress the adult status of a young person, professionals end up excluding parents from any role while still expecting to call on them in an emergency. Far more work needs to be done in enabling parents of children with complex needs to define their own role as their child begins to become an adult.

Cultural issues concerning the transition of people with complex needs

Young people with complex needs who come from an ethnic minority group can face particular issues. Concepts of adolescence and adulthood vary significantly from one culture to another and this will inevitably affect the process of transition. There are also particular issues for young people who might belong to one family culture but who have incorporated certain aspects of a different culture through their peer group and education. While these complexities are to some extent accepted by professionals working with non-disabled ethnic groups, there is often an assumption that all young people with complex needs have exactly the same transition needs regardless of their ethnicity.

Opportunities after school

Currently the options for young people with complex learning difficulties leaving school are limited and geographically variable. The Further Education

Funding Council, which funds the majority of post-school education, will only fund provision for students with learning difficulties that will enable students to progress towards an accredited or vocational course. Different colleges interpret this criterion in very different ways and, while some have full-time courses for young people with complex learning difficulties, others have no such provision.

The Code of Practice emphasises the need for young people to have information on a range of options so that they can make an informed choice. In reality the dearth of options for people with complex needs in many parts of the country can result in a resigned attitude along the lines of 'of course he/she will go on to provision x'.

Inter-agency collaboration

When young people with complex needs become 18, they move from the children and families service to the adult community service in social services. In health services, too, a young person moves from having received physiotherapy and speech therapy, for example, through paediatric services delivered at their school to a situation where they have to be referred to specialist services. This move, from a school that served as a focus point for all services to a situation where services are dislocated, can be particularly difficult for young people who have complex needs. Everybody accepts that young people with complex needs require close collaboration between agencies if their support is to be delivered in the most effective way. However, this seldom happens for a variety of reasons:

- while it is a requirement to invite social services to the transition review, there is not the same requirement to invite a health representative, so this very important area is often not considered in the transition programme
- it is unclear who should be responsible for negotiation in making decisions about joint funded provision, e.g. when a young person has been accepted

onto a residential education course but it is felt that social services should pay for the 'care' element of the package

- agencies tend to organise workloads as if work took place solely within their own agency, hence time is not allocated for essential inter-agency meetings – including the transition review

- there are cultural differences between agencies, which make cross-communication difficult. Health, social services and education agencies work according to different definitions of disability. Also, services tend to gather information according to their own categories (e.g. physical disability, learning difficulty, etc.) or their own eligibility criteria (e.g. banding according to levels of dependency). The reality of this for people with complex needs is that their needs are often not looked at holistically, with them at the centre, but are divided up according to the requirements of particular agencies.

Young people who wish to move on to residential college

There is a particular issue about young people leaving school who wish to move on to residential specialist college. Currently, the Further Education Funding Council will only fund a residential placement if it can be proved that the local further education college cannot provide a suitable placement. This rule is often implemented in a way that is demoralising for the young person, for example they can be asked to obtain 'rejections' from two local colleges. This goes against the Code of Practice recommendation that the young person's views should be at the centre of the process.

The careers service

Specialist careers officers can provide very effective guidance and impartial advice for young people with complex needs during their transition from school. They should be able to have an objective picture of the situation and look further than the immediate next stage. However, there are certain cases in which individuals can be denied access to this support. For instance, young people who have complex needs and have been at a residential school may wish to return to their home area when they leave school. However, they can be denied access to effective guidance in their home area because careers services are no longer allowed to operate outside their home area and so cannot give young people local guidance while they are attending the residential school.

Transition as an on-going process

Young people with complex needs may well take longer to make the transition to a more independent adult life than their non-disabled peers. It is essential that their transition should be looked at in relation to the stage a person has reached and not solely according to chronological age. However, services and structures tend to be established more rigidly than this. There is often a real gap for young people with complex needs who might leave school at 19 and be accepted onto an educational course but require guidance when it finishes two years later. There is no equivalent to a transition plan for these young people; nor do they necessarily have access to specialist careers guidance as the careers service is supposed to work predominantly with young people up to the age of 19.

Examples of good practice

Some of the difficulties listed above require policy change if they are to be rectified. Others have resource implications. However, there are examples of good practice within the current framework.

Design for a successful transition planning programme

A forthcoming FEDA publication[1] has drawn up guidelines for what should be included in a successful transition plan.

Transition planning programme

A successful transition planning programme should include the following elements.

For the young person
A well structured careers education and guidance programme, including:

- the opportunity to visit a range of post-school provision to reach an understanding of the range of opportunities that may be available without the pressure of assessment – at least two years before school leaving
- taster days and link courses in the penultimate school year
- a developing process of careers guidance and action planning, starting with the first transition review in year 9, enabling the young person to assess the options against their own skills and support needs and contribute to the decision-making process
- on-going careers advice and guidance.

For parents/carers:
- early accessible information about the range of options
- clear information about transition planning, guidance and how the process of assessing options fits into this
- an explanation of the roles of the different professionals who will be involved
- a key link person
- availability of an advocate.

For the school and supporting professionals:
- a shared understanding of transition planning and the assessment process, its goals and placement criteria
- an agreed timetable and process of co-operative working
- a clear understanding of professional roles
- an agreement about the information needed to facilitate assessment and how this will be shared.

For college staff:
- an agreed procedure for contributing to the transition planning process, including key contacts
- clarity about information required from the college about the provision and support available
- an agreement about the content of information to go to the college about potential students and the timescale.

Inter-agency transition plans

Some local authorities have developed very effective inter-agency transition plans. Two examples are Oxfordshire and Hackney in Central London.

Oxfordshire

In Oxfordshire the Health Authority, the Education Service and Social Services have worked together to produce an integrated assessment document. This has been implemented across Oxfordshire as the process for transition planning. Young people and their parents find this document particularly useful as it enables them to play a central part in the planning process and to have useful and practical documentation that they can hand on to other services. It also enables parents to distinguish between those parts of the transition process that are going smoothly and those that need extra enquiries or resources. Adult Joint Commissioning Services also find the format and information very useful for their care management and future planning.

To order a copy of the *Oxfordshire Integrated Assessment Manual* and a report on the project contact: Integrated Assessment, Pupil Services, Macclesfield House, New Road, Oxford OX1 1NA. Tel: 01865 810541

Hackney

Hackney's transition plan takes the form of an A4 book with a simple and accessible design. It clearly states the rights of a young disabled person and explains the duties of each agency. It then lists all the local organisations, both statutory and voluntary, that might be able to give support to young people as they move from school. The second part of the document consists of a simple but focused form, with sections to be completed by the young person and by relevant professionals using the information that emerges at the young person's transition review. Sections include:

- issues arising out of the review that are relevant to progression

- social and leisure activities
- health issues
- social services
- future education/training
- housing
- other.

Funding to create the Hackney document came from a post jointly funded by Education, Health and Social Services. Those working in Hackney say that the publication has been warmly welcomed – especially by parents of young people. They also report that the inter-agency transition planning form has clearly helped the transition of young people with more complex needs.

For information and to obtain a copy of Hackney's document, contact: Special Needs Section, Hackney Social Services, Edith Cavell Centre, Enfield Road, London N1 5BA. Tel: 020 8356 7528; fax: 020 8356 7513

Transition workers

Some local authorities employ transition officers whose roles are specifically to co-ordinate and monitor the transition of young people with learning difficulties and/or disabilities. In some cases, this post is funded by the local education authority and in others by social services.

The way in which the work is carried out varies from authority to authority but it is apparent that where there is a named individual to co-ordinate the work and liaise between different services and individuals the transition process is greatly enhanced for the young person.

Action 19+

Action 19+ was specifically set up to try to improve the transition process for disabled people aged over 19 years. It is a consortium that brings together a number of disability organisations.

Action 19+ aims to provide individuals and groups with campaigning information to help them get what they are entitled to. It does this by:

- providing an Action 19+ Guide, which gives advice on how you can get what you want from your local authority
- producing a twice-yearly newsletter, which updates members on new legislation as well as giving examples of good practice
- running workshops and giving presentations across the country.

Action 19+ is based at Scope, 6 Market Road, London N7 9PW. Tel: 020 7619 7251

Post-school education research project

SKILL (the National Bureau for Students with Disabilities) and the University of Cambridge School of Education have recently been successful in gaining National Lottery Funding to run a three-year research project into post-school education for adults with profound and complex learning difficulties.

The project will begin with a period of desk research and a survey of current provision for adults with complex needs. It will then continue with an 18-month period of action research based on four sites. The work is based on the principles of:

- discovering what new opportunities can be created
- making sure that people's own wishes and needs are heard
- finding out the best ways of organising these opportunities
- working with all support services.

The project will produce a report for policy-makers and managers and a multi-modal pack of materials for practitioners. During the final stages of the project, there will be a nine-month period of dissemination involving staff development.

For more details and to be put on a mailing list, contact: School of Education, University of Cambridge, Shaftesbury Road, Cambridge CB2 4DP. Fax: 01223 324421

Reference

1. Faraday S, Maudslay L, Palmer M, Richardson S. *Assessing for placement at specialist colleges.* London: FEDA, forthcoming.

Further reading

City and Hackney Joint Finance. *Leaving School, Opportunities for young people in Hackney.*

DFEE. *Code of Practice on the Identification and Assessment of Special Educational Needs.*

Disabled Persons (Services, Consultation and Representation) Act 1986.

Morris J. *Move On Up: supporting young disabled people in their transition to adulthood.* London: Barnardos, 1999.

Morris J. *Hurtling into a Void, Transition to adulthood for young disabled people with 'complex health and support needs'.* Brighton: Pavilion Publishing Ltd, 1999.

Pearson M *et al. Positive health in transition. A guide to effective and reflective transition planning for young people with learning disabilities.* Manchester: National Development Team, 1999.

SKILL. *Successful Transitions, Implementing Sections 5 and 6 of the Disabled Persons (Services, Consultation and Representation) Act 1986.* London: SKILL, 1997.

Contacts

SKILL (National Bureau for Students with Disabilities), Chapter House, 18–20 Crucifix Lane, London, SE1 3JW. Tel: 020 4750 0620; freephone information service: 0800 328 5050; fax: 020 7450 0650. e-mail: info@skill.org.uk

Chapter 7

Supported employment – including everyone[*]

Becoming an employee can affect positively the way people with learning difficulties view themselves, building their confidence and self-esteem. Becoming a paid worker and contributing member of society can also change the way their family and peer group see them.

Employment opportunities must become a part of the mainstream support offered to men and women with learning difficulties, not left to small agencies, inadequately funded, on 'the edge' of services. (Days of Change, 1998)

Razia's story

Razia had spent her days in a local authority day centre since leaving school. A young Asian woman in her twenties, she had little clear verbal language and was engaged in very few activities. She seemed to flit from place to place and not stay with anything. She spent much of her time sitting alone, or with her only friend. Others mostly rejected her and she got into fights, some of which were serious. Possessions such as keys or a handbag would go missing, causing her distress and resulting in a bad tempered evening for her family. At home she would sit in the same position, crouched on the floor, her back against the radiator and doing nothing in spite of the exhortations of her family. Life wasn't terribly stimulating for Razia and it was clear that the day centre was not an environment in which she was flourishing. Plans for new-style day services offered an ideal opportunity to think about what she wanted to do with her life.

[*] Dedicated to the memory of Razia Takolia. With thanks and acknowledgement to Carol Munroe Edwards, Katrina Alton, Simon Thorne and Mark Liddle.

> I had no idea if a job was meaningful to Razia, or what she could do,
> let alone if she wanted to work. For a year, I didn't work with her,
> repeating to myself 'it's not that she can't work – I just don't know
> how to do this yet'.

Supported employment assumes that people with disabilities, including those with the label of severe disability, have 'the capacity to work … if appropriate, on-going support can be provided'.[1]

Seeing someone's potential

How do you know if someone wants to work? The first step is learning how to 'listen'. People have many more ways to communicate than with words. We need to use our eyes, our imagination, our intelligence and intuition to be aware of all the ways that a person says 'I want to do something more with my life'. A person with a complex disability may not be able to express in words that she/he wants a job, or know what a job means. However, boredom, frustration, depression and challenging behaviours can be real clues to a need for a valued role, a purpose, activity or even structure. Someone may have an interest in all that's new or in every new person that arrives. A job could really satisfy a craving for learning or curiosity. Real pleasure taken in particular activities could indicate potential enjoyment of a similar sort of work. A desire for order or routine may be well-met in particular sorts of job tasks.

'Don't forget me!'

Although Razia didn't have the words to say 'I want a job', she never let me forget that she was there when I visited her day centre, appearing immediately by my side, with a questioning tone in her voice. I felt she was saying, 'don't forget me!' as her peers left for jobs of their own. Her desperation and keenness made a big impact on me. I felt she wanted to do something – I just didn't know what.

Thinking about what works – profiling

The most important thing is to find out what 'sparks' the person – what gives him or her a buzz. When and where does she/he seem most alive and animated? Motivation is the best indicator for employment success, not ability. It's a lot easier to teach a skill than to change an attitude. It is vital to get to know people well, spending time with the person in their usual settings and doing a few things together in the community.

Getting to know a person for employment – profiling – means trying to get the right questions answered. It means not giving up until you have a real sense of what matters to this individual. The TSI Vocational Profile[2] and John O'Brien's Personal Profile[3] are invaluable tools to help focus a thoughtful enquiry. What does the person like to do? What is important to the person? What works (and doesn't work) for the person? Is the person attracted to particular things (pens, paper, machines) or environments (indoors/ outdoors, quiet/noisy)? Who does the person like to be with? What do other people get out of being with this person? There are all sorts of clues to be gathered about jobs that could work.

The profile is not a form to fill in, but rather a place to capture on-going relevant information. It culminates in the description of an 'ideal job' or a desirable future. An ideal job will meet someone's motivation. The next challenge is to make a job-match, and brainstorm real jobs and employers that may fit the bill.

A love of learning revealed

I was struggling with where I could go with Razia. Once, at a meeting at my office, I attempted to find out more about what work she might be good at by passing her a duster. She passed it back to me, in disgust. I was learning about her motivation! During my visits to the day centre, I noticed that Razia often held a piece of paper and a pen in her hand.

I had a hunch that she might enjoy things to do with paper, even if she didn't write.

My colleague, Carol, tried a day's photocopying in a social services office – which was illuminating. Razia was totally absorbed in the task, concentrating hard and fascinated by all the different functions of this complex machine. We saw how much she loved learning and how engaged she was in the activity. We began to look in earnest for office related work.

Making real life choices

If you've had very few life experiences, it's practically impossible to know what you want to do, let alone try to communicate that. A person with complex needs may have had very few opportunities to make any important decisions about their life.

Trying out things may be vital, and personal experience is the best way to make a meaningful choice. Setting up a job taster in different workplaces may help the person – and you – find out what works. Job tasters should be strictly time-limited and have clear goals. A job analysis,[4] with tasks and support, should be clearly thought out before the job taster starts.

It is vital to learn how the person says *no* and how she/he expresses discomfort, displeasure or indicates that there is a problem.

Mailing, clipping, pasting, copying and making friends

Razia did a work taster in a mailing services organisation. Our goals were to discover if she really wanted to work and for her to learn some specific new tasks. Razia said 'no' very clearly, and if she didn't want to do something, she wouldn't do it. We figured that if Razia wanted to go to work every day, then it meant that she was enjoying it and that she wanted to do it. In the event, Razia hardly missed a day. Her family reported that they had not seen her so keen to go out for a long time. She'd get ready long before her Dial-a-Ride bus arrived. She learned lots of new skills, including cutting and pasting policy cuttings, and sorting out *Guardian* crossword competitions by differentiating between different patterns. She made friends and enjoyed the new experience of being respected and liked, becoming very close to another colleague, Josey. She proved herself to be a hard working, motivated, enthusiastic and popular team member – a long way from her experience in the day centre.

Team working

It is important to get the support of colleagues and other people who know the person well: creative sessions throwing ideas around can produce brainwaves; stories can give insight and inspire. It is important to share problems, to keep from getting stuck. Inspiration and help may come in the form of a speech and language therapist, a sister or a brother, care manager, occupational therapist, colleagues in related agencies ... . Don't be afraid to ask for help and treat new challenges as welcome opportunities for learning.

Employers

If you are an employer, there is no more powerful message to other employers than creating job opportunities – especially if you represent one of the largest employers in the area (the local authority and the health authority). Identify tasks that could be delegated or carved out of an existing role – perhaps highly paid staff spend a lot of time photocopying? Perhaps some tasks never get done? Write a supported employment policy to complement the equal opportunities policy of your organisation and use recruitment to implement it. By showing this leadership, you blaze a trail for working with other local employers.

If, on the other hand, you are helping people to get jobs, call employers up and go to see them at their workplaces. Approach them in the spirit of enquiry, experiment and partnership. Find out more about the different jobs and tasks involved. Ask to do a job analysis. Explain the particular projects that your team are working on and ask for the employers' support. It is all right to say to an employer, 'this is an aspect of our work we're developing and we'd really like to ask for your input as a community employer'. Benefits to them could include being seen as taking equal opportunities seriously; co-workers may have family members with a disability. There may be a task that is not getting done, or that is hard to recruit for, or that would be better delegated. Accuracy may be more important than speed. Perhaps there is a friendly employer you could approach who could help you to talk to other employers. Employers often want to employ people with disabilities but are not sure how to do so effectively. You don't need flashy literature – an employer is buying you. Your understanding of their business and the person you represent are what counts. It is exciting, it is breaking new ground – and the employers could be your partners.

Headhunted

Razia's placement came to an end and left those involved in her support totally committed to finding paid work for her. Her team at this point included a very committed care manager, an imaginative community resource worker who had supported her successfully in a mainstream women's art class and an Asian disability outreach worker. Her family was more sceptical and it took a lot of confidence in what Razia was saying to continue. We made a video as a record of her achievements for her family.

Razia had even convinced the local disability employment adviser that working was not only important and meaningful to her, but that she had a lot to contribute. Razia was eventually headhunted by the mail services organisation when a paid job vacancy came up some months later, much to her joy and pride.

Support

One-to-one, individualised support is the key to ensuring success. It is important to ensure that support can be on-going for as long as necessary. Staff need the skills to teach effectively. Without these elements, supported employment and a life in the community become but distant dreams.

When teaching a skill, the job coach aims to gradually 'fade out' as the person becomes confident and competent at their task. Some additional assistance may always be required, for example needing help with putting on and taking off a coat. This additional assistance can come in various forms (see *Keys to the Workplace*[5] for lots of ideas) and may be about negotiating within a workplace (is there a co-worker who could help?). However, some on-going assistance from a paid worker may be always needed. This does not invalidate the benefit of the person working and should be realised as an essential strategy to make inclusion work for all members of the community. Support may also be about negotiating changes to the way work is organised or carried out in the workplace ('reasonable accommodation' is a legal requirement for employers under the Disability Discrimination Act 1997) or about making use of assistive technology. However, changes to a workplace should not be sought until natural methods are exhausted.

Benefits of inclusion – a chance for self-reinvention

A different woman

So, what did having a job mean to Razia's life? She loved mailing work and tackled her job with gusto. She was proud of herself, and loved what her new income could buy: smart, trendy rucksacks, pretty jewellery and music. She had a renewed confidence and self-esteem. She made friends who cared deeply about her and who trooped in to hospital when she was seriously ill. Her family, who had found it hard to believe what a different person Razia could be away from home, became

very proud that she was earning money and were pleased by how happy
she was. She no longer came home in bad moods. She never had a
problem getting on with other people in the community, unlike at the
day centre.

One of the greatest strengths of supported employment is the liberating
opportunity it offers a person to reinvent him or herself. New opportunities
give a person the chance to be perceived afresh and without baggage, and to
experience him or herself in a brand new way. Labels can be shed, valued
roles, respect and affection gained.

Changing days, changing lives

Razia's life changed radically from her limiting days at the centre –
to a life fashioned by her own interests and desires. She attended a
mosaic course with a mainstream class at college, supported by her
community resource worker. A woman with a huge zest for life had
emerged from someone determined that *something* was going to happen.
There were lots of benefits, for lots of people, from Razia leading a
spirited life in the world at large.

If you have commissioning responsibility for ensuring employment support
for people with learning difficulties, the following pointers to achieving
inclusion for people with more complex disabilities may be helpful.

Managers' checklist

- Organise funding for supported employment so that people with severe and complex disabilities are included. This may be specified by commissioners, care managers or stated in contracts or service agreements
- Re-provision services to have the scope to offer one-to-one support for individuals in the community
- Ensure that appropriate, skilled support can be provided for the person by building funding around the realistic support that a person may need
- Be aware that outcomes may take longer to achieve, and that on-going support may be required to ensure a successful outcome
- Seek good quality profiles as part of a contract or commission
- Be aware that very few people remain in their first job. People with severe disabilities have just the same right to get bored with their jobs, or to not get on with their boss, as anyone else! Everyone needs to have the possibility of moving on
- Designate jobs or carve a job from existing tasks
- Write a supported employment policy for your organisation
- Access mainstream employment and training monies – employment outcomes that you create in your organisation will count towards your borough's regeneration targets
- Ensure that staff get the support and training they need to carry out the work – training in systematic instruction is highly recommended, not only for teaching skills, but also for profiling and decision-making. Mentoring between organisations may bring in fresh impetus and ideas. Encourage a learning culture
- Ensure good joint working between health, social services, and the voluntary sector
- Make the most of other resources, such as the Employment Service and the Disability Service Teams. Circles of support could be a useful source of encouragement, ideas and networking

Summary

Don't try to change the world on your own – get help. Work as a team and find someone you can throw ideas around with. Find other people who know the person you are trying to help well and who can offer insights or tell stories that can help give ideas. Start small – work with one or two people with complex disabilities to start with. Get the support of a friendly employer who is open to sharing a journey of discovery. Don't be afraid to say, 'we're learning how to do this and experimenting with what works – we'd really like your help with this project'.

The most important thing to do is to listen to the person. Be imaginative and creative, experiment, and keep trying – say you don't know how to do something yet, rather than someone can't work.

Postscript

This reflection has poignancy as, sadly, Razia died last year from kidney failure. She experienced difficulties accessing the primary health care she needed, not only because of her communication and other disabilities but also because of her ethnicity. Neither she nor her family spoke English as a first language, and she didn't have a health advocate. The combination of cultural issues and disability, as well as class and gender, can make access to health care particularly problematic for some groups of people.

References

1. Definition of supported employment from the AFSE (Association for Supported Employment).
2. Developed in the UK by Training in Systematic Instruction (TSI) Ltd, which runs training courses on the teaching and organisational skills around developing employment for people with severe disabilities.
3. O'Brien J. Personal Profile. In: *Framework for Accomplishment.* Atlanta: Response Systems Associates, 1991.
4. Developed by TSI Ltd.
5. Callahan MJ and Garner B. *Keys to the Workplace: Skills and Supports for People with Disabilities.* Baltimore, MD: Paul H Brookes Publishing Co., 1997.

Further reading

Flippo K, Inge K and Barcus M. *Assistive Technology – A Resource for School, Work and the Community.* Baltimore, MD: Paul H Brookes Publishing Co., 1995.

Contacts

Association for Supported Employment, Pennine View, Gamblesby, Penrith CA10 1HR. Tel: 01768 881225; e-mail: afse@Onyxnet.co.uk; web site: http://web.onyx.net.co.uk/afse- onyx.net.co.uk

National Development Team, St Peter's Court, 8 Trumpet Street, Manchester M1 5LW. Tel: 0161 228 7055; fax: 0161 228 7059; e-mail: office@ndt.org.uk

Training in Systematic Instruction Ltd, c/o Ashleigh, Sunnyside, Todmorden, Lancashire OL14 7AP. Tel: 01706 813555; e-mail: tsi@ncr1.poptel.org.uk

Chapter 8

Looking for leisure inclusion

Inclusion is not just about 'being in' the community; more importantly it is about being able to participate actively in it. It is about creating opportunities for individuals to be included and also about how the community itself adapts to become more inclusive to disadvantaged people.

It is essential to influence generic services at the local level: to work with housing, employment, education, leisure and other services to help them recognise the need for accessibility, challenge their own discrimination, and create new opportunities for people. (Days of Change, 1998)

Background

Newham Leisure Services department provides opportunities for all its citizens through a wide range of operations, including leisure centres, parks and gardens, play provision, libraries, sports development, museums, a farm, a zoo, water sports centre and nature reserve, arts and events. Throughout the year, there is a continuous programme of activities and events, which take place both within purpose-built facilities and in community settings. In addition, there is a large grants budget to encourage and support leisure provision in the voluntary sector. For example, the famous Theatre Royal at Stratford East has been a successful leisure partner for many years.

Newham Council has an on-going programme of investing in new leisure developments. A riverside park, multipurpose leisure centre and new arts and performance complex are all due to open over the next year. The Council has a deep commitment to encouraging local people to use, enjoy and benefit from their leisure facilities.

The current scene

Traditionally, Newham's service developments for disabled people have concentrated on improving physical access to facilities and providing 'special' programmes, particularly through multi-activity sessions in leisure centres. These sessions mainly cater for people using day care centres in the Borough and include people both with learning difficulties and more complex needs.

A young man with complex needs who uses a wheelchair expressed interest in gardening. A local garden centre got involved but needed to make some alterations to fit in with his needs. Now there are plans to make the centre accessible for anyone with disabilities.

There are areas of good inclusionary practice in the Leisure department, such as the *PlayBarn*, which is a specially-designed and fully integrated out-of-school play service, and a parks gardening project that is managed by a group of local residents including people with learning difficulties. However, managers feel that there is a considerable way to go before they can demonstrate that main services are really addressing social inclusiveness.

The second phase of the Changing Days project challenged this segregated approach and provided an ideal opportunity to test the department's understanding and current ability to embrace 'inclusion'.

Working with Changing Days

On the face of it, the requirements of the project seemed relatively simple. Four of the 13 project participants had expressed a wish, through their personal planning circles, to take part in more activities in leisure centres. However, it was not possible for Leisure Services to fulfil these people's wishes as smoothly and quickly as they would have wished: the project was well under way when Leisure Services became involved and they had no previous experience of the person-centred planning approach. This meant that important learning and preparation time, which was needed for the service and its staff and which in theory could have been usefully employed at an earlier stage, was lost.

The following points summarise the main difficulties that arose during the project:

- leisure managers and staff expressed fears about their lack of skills in providing physical assistance and personal care to people with multiple disabilities
- staff also expressed their lack of confidence in communicating effectively with people with learning difficulties and/or sensory disabilities
- there was some concern that other customers might complain or cause unpleasantness in integrated settings
- there were gaps in internal communications among centre staff, which resulted in failures to anticipate a participant's particular needs when he or she visited
- carers and social workers did not always keep in touch with the participating leisure staff to include them in the person-centred planning or maintain continuity in planned arrangements
- attending personal care staff did not always consciously help the leisure staff to get to know the participant.

Some of these issues were successfully addressed, which did improve the leisure experience for the participants. This was enabled, in the first place, through the active involvement of the Leisure Policy Development Manager, who was able to engage the interest and commitment of local leisure staff. This resulted in changes being made, such as a hoist at a swimming pool being more readily available and the successful negotiation of provision of a suitable changing area for people with complex needs visiting the pool. Two leisure staff were designated to work with the project and became members of planning circles. The manager also became a planning circle member.

Top tips – helping people with multiple disabilities to take part in leisure

1. There *will* be people in leisure who want to make a difference and who can make change happen. Ideally, but not exclusively, this should be through the active support of the leisure director and other senior leisure officers. Without the endorsement of senior management it is very difficult to get a widescale initiative in place and working well, especially as this will require staffing resources and some cross-agency working

2. If you have no initial point of contact with your local leisure services department, a useful starting point is to check the council's internal telephone for leisure related staff with 'development', 'projects' or 'outreach' in their titles. Very often these post holders have a remit to work on new initiatives and they will make the necessary arrangements with their managers and colleagues. Look out especially for teams with development titles, such as sports development, arts development or parks development

3. Find out about the whole range of activities and opportunities that take place in your local parks, libraries, museums, community centres and play facilities, as well as the more obvious facilities in leisure centres. Contact the different services and get their specific information and publicity. It should be noted that not all leisure activities fall within the scope of a single department in every local authority

4. Include the voluntary sector in your search for appropriate contacts. Most authorities fund local groups where disabled people are made welcome and are fully included in the activities. These groups are often active in the areas of music, arts, performance and crafts, and certainly have been more alive to the ambitions of disabled people than many local authority managed leisure services

5. Involve your key leisure contact(s) early on in the person's planning circle. This will introduce a wider perspective on the local leisure options and allow for some structured planning as to how these can best be accessed. Also, the closer the leisure contacts stay, the more they can learn, share and achieve. Most importantly, they become familiar to the central person and to the principal carers

6. It is important to remember that few leisure staff will have either the experience or training to give physical support to and communicate with people who have complex disabilities or sensory impairments. This is likely to be the case both with the development contacts and service operations staff, e.g. reception, recreation or library assistants. Consider providing some basic training or guidance for involved leisure staff to help them gain skills and confidence

7. The issue of leisure staff expressing fears about competence and confidence needs to be addressed by leisure managers – otherwise they will forever remain barriers to inclusion. It must be the overarching responsibility of the leisure department to ensure a combination of skill training, opportunities for direct experience with people with multiple disabilities and an absolutely clear operating policy in which discrimination and harassment by any person will not be tolerated in leisure facilities

8. Everyone in the planning circle needs to be realistic about leisure participation and its social potential. It takes considerable time and effort in any leisure setting to move from participation to social involvement beyond the bounds of the activity itself. It is crucial that regular attendance can be organised and supported, so experience and familiarity can build a base for possible future social developments

9. Carers or personal care staff do need to involve themselves in the familiarisation of the leisure activity. This presence and active involvement generates confidence in the leisure staff and allows for their learning by example. It is tempting for carers and care staff to consider the leisure session as a respite opportunity when in fact it needs to be spent sharing the best means of communicating with the participant

Conclusion

We should all share an overall plan for person-centred and inclusionary leisure. We should not accept organisational barriers to making leisure accessible and integral to the life of people who have complex needs. All who work in local authority leisure should take a personal role in developing or championing opportunities for inclusion and in seeking out partners who will help us achieve this goal.

Chapter 9

Creative movements in day services

Many men and women with complex needs spend much of the week doubly segregated in special care units based in day centres. Moving from this to supporting each person to participate in the community is often difficult and time-consuming. The good news is that more and more success stories are proving it can be done.

No special buildings, no special places. This feels very difficult because it does not tell us how to replace the existing day service. The answer is, we do not replace it: we start to work differently with people as individuals until we have created a new style of personalised support. (Days of Change, 1998)

Background and history

The Lewisham Intensive Support Resource (ISR) began life in 1995 as a new initiative within Lifestyles, Lewisham Social Care and Health's day services for people with learning difficulties. Lewisham had been providing for people with learning disabilities and complex needs within mainstream day centres and community bases. An outreach team of three day service officers provided specialist support to service users with the highest support needs, but this was limited due to the peripatetic nature of the service.

In 1995 an influx of school leavers with profound learning and multiple disabilities required Lifestyles to plan a new service that could creatively provide for people with increasingly complex needs. Working with Lewisham Partnership, the joint Health and Social Service Commissioners, Lifestyles opened the ISR as a new specialist service integrated within an existing resource centre for service users who have moderate to severe learning difficulties.

The ISR caters for a core group of eight service users and offers outreach support and advice to other people within Lifestyles with similar needs. A team of seven specialist day service officers, a part-time community development worker, a senior co-ordinator and two lunchtime support workers make up the ISR staff group.

Referrals

The ISR receives referrals in the form of community care assessments via district social work teams. Potential service users are then screened against more detailed criteria that use an holistic approach to assess their needs *and* the needs of their carers. Most of the ISR service users have a range of the following disabilities, which means that they require a much higher level of support:

- all members of the group have cerebral palsy and use wheelchairs. Several people have spinal curvatures that affect their posture and can lead to related health problems such as hernias. All need lots of help to move about and make themselves comfortable, using hoists, transfer boards and safe manual handling procedures
- everybody in the core group has epilepsy. Some people are prone to regular seizures and need a lot of support, particularly if they are prone to episodes of status epileptius
- chronic chest problems are common and several people need daily physiotherapy in the form of postural drainage. Close contact with the physiotherapy team is maintained to ensure that people receive a high level of support
- two people often suffer from airway blockages due to the inhalation of food, drink or saliva and the staff team have to administer first aid on a regular basis. The staff team has also supported two people who required tube feeding
- everyone in the group needs careful help with eating and drinking because of swallowing problems, and many are following modified diets with thickened drinks and pureed food

- only one person has a small amount of verbal communication. Other
  people communicate by vocalising, gesturing, body language and facial
  expressions. Several people are now using switches to trigger voice
  messages or yes/no responses. The use of technology is on the increase
  with the support of the speech and language therapy team.

Timetables and activities

The ISR mission statement states that the service aims to 'value each
individual person, exactly as they are', and this approach is a key focus in
the planning of activities. At present the ISR still provides a traditional
9 a.m.–4 p.m. service between Monday and Friday, offering individual
timetables with a variety of activities. In the early days the range of activities
was limited and mainly concentrated on centre-based groups, such as music,
relaxation and massage. Today, however, the staff and service users are
much more experienced and able to try different things, partly due to the
following reasons:

- the whole staff team have put a lot of effort into building strong links
  with community resources such as the bowling alley, the snooker hall,
  leisure centres, education and arts groups. This has led to a slow but
  steady expansion of accessible and appropriate activities away from the
  day centre. The bowling alley has provided special equipment and a
  tournament for people with restricted movements, while the leisure
  centre provides some slots in the new warm hydro pool as a result of
  effective liaison
- the confidence of everyone involved with the ISR – both staff and
  service users – has increased as a result of experience and expertise.
  Everyone is encouraged to log information in a growing library of books,
  files and leaflets. This is a simple but common sense method of ensuring
  that lessons learned, whether positive or negative, do not need to be
  repeated. For example, the swimming file contains background and
  safety information about all the hydro pools used by the ISR, including

risk assessments and guidelines. Similarly, the community access files contain hundreds of leaflets about interesting places to visit in and around London and vital information about their facilities and accessibility

- every September there is a major review of each service user's programme. Consultation takes place using a variety of methods and results in an holistic overview of individual preferences. People are consulted face-to-face about what they have enjoyed and what they would like to change. Keyworkers take a lead in the timetable review by keeping daily monitoring sheets about their key clients' activities and progress. Parents and carers are also consulted, either at the centre or at home (as some service users feel more able to make a choice or to voice an opinion at home)

- the keyworker and the senior co-ordinator collate the evidence. The individual timetable review sheets then shape the overall timetable for the ISR service. Compromises have to be negotiated, as one-to-one staffing levels are not always available, particularly as some activities such as swimming require a two-to-one ratio.

The ISR timetable follows community education term dates and breaks for Christmas, Easter and summer programmes. Though the service is open during these periods, the thrice-annual 'holiday' periods allow for natural breaks and a review period for staff and service users. At the end of every term, the timetable is reviewed using the above methods and changes take place accordingly.

In recent years, the ISR team has concentrated on building up information on each service user so that their choices and preferences in life are accessible and respected by all those who support them. With the help of speech and language therapists, keyworkers help service users build up on-going profiles of themselves, their likes and dislikes, their progress and achievements. These profiles can take several different forms.

One person uses a laptop computer to input photos of his favourite pop stars and photos and voices of his family. He can press a switch connected to the headrest on his wheelchair to trigger the audio-visual effects. Together with his keyworker he aims to build up more information about his life, particularly about how he likes to be supported to eat and drink, how he communicates, and valuable information about himself that he wants to share with others.

Other people have communication passports in the form of photo albums, with photos of the things that matter to them, however big or small. The photos and accompanying text can capture moments that are difficult to express in words alone. They allow people to let others know about their needs, their likes and dislikes, dreams and favourite pastimes.

One service user has a photo of the habitual hand movements he makes when he is upset and wants to be left alone; other photos and text describe how he likes to make croaky sounds with his voice and usually enjoys it if people echo his sounds back to him. Pictures are included of his family and key people and places in his life. There are also photos of the position he is most comfortable in when eating and which illustrate how he can hold his own spoon with the correct support.

The text is written in the first person, which has the powerful effect of giving people a voice. For example:

- 'If I'm upset about something I might cry out, and I will also rub my left hand on my face and move about a lot in my chair.'
- 'When I make a humming sound and bite my sleeve it usually means that I am happy and relaxed. If I'm really happy I will put my arms round the neck of someone I know really well, and I like them to rock me and we have a lovely cuddle.'

- 'I need you to tell me whenever you are about to move me in my wheelchair because I can't see where I'm going. I also like it if you pat my left shoulder to turn left and my right shoulder to turn right.'
- 'I am much happier sitting with my back towards the wall so I can see everyone when I'm eating my dinner or having a drink. If I've got a good view I don't need to move my head about so I can enjoy my food much more.'

These valuable insights into service users' lives are collated from the views and observations of those who know them well: mothers, fathers, keyworkers and other ISR or residential staff, and anyone else who can share their impression of what the service user wants and needs from life. Service users can take their communication passports with them to respite care placements, which can make transitions and handover of information much smoother and more personal.

In addition to communication passports, service users also have personal folders and lockers where they can keep objects of reference, certificates of achievements, personal video recordings or audiocassettes and other items that are personal to them.

Individual planning

Individual planning meetings take place every six months. Over the past few years, the shape and form of these meetings have evolved to involve service users on a more accessible level. In the past, meetings tended to be health-biased, with an emphasis on such things as mobility issues and eating/drinking problems. Social workers, speech therapists, physiotherapists and occupational therapists were invited as a matter of course. Now keyworkers and the ISR co-ordinator spend time thinking about who the client may *really* want at their meeting, and consult the service user and his/her parent or carer. Other family members and friends are welcome to attend if it is felt this is respecting the service user's wishes. Rather than holding meetings with ten or so professionals, people are invited to attend a relevant part of the meeting or to submit a report. A recent meeting was attended by a service user's taxi driver, as someone who plays an active and valuable role in the client's everyday life. He has become a good friend and was able to make a positive contribution to the meeting from a different perspective.

Before an individual planning meeting, keyworkers spend time filming different aspects of their key clients' activities so that *their* video can then be shown during *their* meeting. Video is a simple method of relaxing the formal meeting environment and can both illustrate agenda items for the service user and enlighten other people. It is also an objective method of capturing important aspects of people's lives. Recently, a service user took part in and won a prize in a London-wide bowling competition. This was a great achievement for her as previously, though she enjoyed going to the bowling alley, she only watched from the side. A new bowling alley with adapted equipment meant she could bowl by herself, and she was able to show her winning moment to her parents on the video.

Meetings are no longer restricted to the centre: if a service user and parent/carer are happier at home, then the ISR will accommodate this. It is often found that everyone is more relaxed in the home environment.

The ISR has developed and piloted a new Lifestyles format for individual planning meetings, which places an emphasis on timetables and activities. This means that discussions and decisions can be fed back into the termly timetable reviews. The agenda is flexible but ensures that a service user doesn't end up with a list of goals such as 'wheelchair brakes need attending to' or 'guidelines for eating and drinking need to be reviewed'. Important as these issues are, it is felt that they shouldn't dominate and suffocate somebody's aims and aspirations for the next six months or longer. The final section of an individual planning meeting is entitled 'Dreams and Wishes'. This is a chance for the service user and those who support him/her to think of one or two positive, exciting things they would like to try in the next six months.

Health

As described already, everybody who attends the ISR needs a lot of help every day with their particular health needs. This means that the service must be flexible and creative. The following are some of the methods that the ISR team has developed to ensure that service users' health needs are met, without dominating people's lives.

Daily timetables and routines are liable to be altered at the last minute. Sudden changes in people's health needs can mean that an activity needs to be postponed or altered because they are simply not well enough. A health problem for one particular person may impact on other groups or individuals because the two-to-one staff ratio needed for immediate chest physio, for example, can take staff away from another activity.

Any groups or individuals working in partnership with the ISR need to be fully briefed about the kind of unforeseen events that can occur. They need to be aware that joint work can mean moving at a different pace because of transport problems or someone's health or mood on a given day. Although not necessarily slowing things down, this does mean that contingency plans are required in case things do need to change suddenly. External community or education workers need to be guided by ISR staff until they have built up relationships with service users. For example, the background knowledge of an established member of the ISR team may clarify that what might seem like only a small step forward for a service user could actually be a major achievement. The two sides need to work together to make sure that successes are recognised and celebrated.

The ISR staff team frequently need to deal with episodes of airway blockages and severe epileptic seizures, and need support to build up and maintain confidence, skills and knowledge. Debriefing support after dealing with a life-threatening incident is very important to analyse the risks and enable staff to raise concerns and receive feedback.

Guidelines and risk assessments are used to ensure there is a balance of risk-taking *and* quality of life for all the service users who attend the ISR. The support of the Lewisham Community Team for Adults with Learning Disabilities is welcomed, and parents and carers are involved throughout. For example, all service users need guidelines for eating and drinking. These are written by keyworkers and/or the senior co-ordinator and based on the written and verbal reports from speech and language therapists.

Managing risk

One service user with particularly complex health problems originally had a set of guidelines that stated he needed two staff present when he was out in the community, in case he experienced any major problems. Although these were helpful and appropriate when he first came to the ISR, as people got to know him better it became clear that the guidelines were restricting him. He couldn't easily go out for a quick walk to get some fresh air or pop down to the shops to buy himself some lunch without operational and staffing issues impacting on his choice. A multidisciplinary risk assessment took place, and his mother was consulted. This resulted in revised guidelines, which meant he could go out in the local area with only one person to support him. The key risk-reduction factors included the staff member taking a mobile telephone and a contact card to hand to members of the public in case of an airway blockage. It also required the support staff to make a quick and very general assessment of the person's health before leaving the building. If the service user was particularly chesty or seemed unusually under the weather, he would not go out without more support.

The support staff need to know what is the norm for each service user and exactly *when* there is a need for further action or medical intervention. It can be a *very* fine line, particularly as the staff cannot expect to have the years of intuitive knowledge of a parent and are *not* medically trained or qualified. The ISR team often have to decide whether or not to call an ambulance. They have to balance the chance that they may be whisked off to A&E unnecessarily against not acting and putting someone at risk because there really is a need for urgent medical help. A common scenario has been that the service user waits around for several hours at the hospital and then is sent home without treatment. More recently, ambulance staff have been happy to assess the service user at the centre and have carried out suction and given a small amount of oxygen on site. They have relied on the support staff's knowledge that the client appears to have recovered and doesn't need to be admitted to the hospital. This has only happened in the presence of a manager and staff with several years of knowledge of a particular client. If in *any* doubt, staff are advised and reassured about not taking risks, and instructed to seek appropriate medical help for the service user.

Community links and partnerships

Over the past four years, the ISR has built up a whole range of fruitful links in the local community and these continue to grow.

The Drake Music Project, based in Greenwich, is a national charity that provides creative opportunities for people with disabilities to use computers and technology. Drake has worked with the ISR for three years, and since 1997, has provided a weekly workshop for people with profound and multiple learning disabilities. Use of the Drake technology has gone hand in hand with increased use of electronic switches and devices in the ISR. So, where a service user has been learning to press a switch with his head to indicate yes or no, he has also had the opportunity to use his switch to trigger sounds within a musical setting. The Drake tutor has learned from ISR service users and staff, and vice-versa. Now the group works on termly musical projects. The project for the autumn term 1999 was based on the theme of transport and journeys. The service users recorded the sounds and voices they heard on their journey to the Drake workshop and built up a piece of music around these sounds.

The link with the Drake Music Project has led to another successful partnership during the past 18 months. IMPRO (Integrated Music Project) is a voluntary organisation, running a three-year music project in south east London. The emphasis is on developing musical communities by running training groups for community music workshop leaders and by providing residencies in schools and community music groups. IMPRO have provided two term-long residencies with the ISR and the Drake project. This has led to four ISR service users taking part in two large-scale performances. For the most recent performance, professional musicians worked alongside the ISR/Drake group on two pieces. The challenge was to find a way of making sure the performance worked, even if the service users weren't in the mood or healthy enough to take part on the night. With the backing of the school music groups, the professional musicians, the Drake technology and an extremely creative approach from IMPRO, the ISR performers coped really well with such a big event. One of the pieces included a rap that the school children chanted to introduce each of the ISR performers by name, and their switch-operated music. This meant the service users and their music were immediately recognisable by an audience and also that they had an audible and very rigorous musical cue about when it was time to press their switch. Each person 'owned' their sounds that they had chosen and worked on throughout the term, but if they couldn't perform on the night for whatever reason, the show still went on, thanks to the technology.

At the first performance, one of the service users became quite upset, overwhelmed by the lights, the audience and the different atmosphere, and couldn't take part. After a while he took part in his own way by dancing at the side with two of the ISR team, and by his contribution being acknowledged by the compere over the PA. Before the next performance, IMPRO organised an extra rehearsal day to give everyone a chance to acclimatise to the noisy environment. All the participants had a chance to get to know each other, which meant that the performance day was more relaxed for everyone. An ISR representative visited the schools beforehand to talk to the children about the ISR performers and explain how the technology worked. The children had a chance to ask straightforward questions about disability issues, without putting anybody in an uncomfortable position. It also meant they were quite ready and willing to be friendly and welcoming to the ISR users. The result was very positive – *and* good fun.

The final example shows the ISR being opportunistic and taking the initiative. Community Education Lewisham (CEL) were due to close one of their classes for people with special needs due to lack of attendance. The ISR pointed out there were no adult education classes that specifically looked at the needs of people with profound learning disabilities. CEL agreed to use the funding from the other class to open one aimed at people with more complex needs. The ISR team came up with a name, 'Getting To Know You', and wrote a term plan. The class is held in a CEL building used by other students for a range of adult education classes. The aim of the class is to concentrate on group and self-awareness. One week the class may be taking photos of each other in fancy dress, looking in mirrors and then creating collages from the photos and out of different textured materials. The next week they might all meet up in a café and exchange news about their week. The tutor comes from a creative background and has taken over the planning of activities, with the input of everyone else present. The class is now over-subscribed and is popular amongst both service users and staff from the ISR, as well as other people with similar needs from other parts of the Borough.

Future plans

With the numbers of school leavers with complex needs on the increase, it is likely that the ISR will expand or act as a model for a 'sister' service in the next year or so. There is already a waiting list of people who require the kind of intensive input that the ISR can give. Above all, any similar service needs to be creative and organised, and needs to be excited about the endless possibilities that *are* out there for people with multiple disabilities.

Chapter 10

Keeping users central – working together in groups

Achieving effective partnership with men and women with learning difficulties requires a change in the service culture so that it is seen as everyone's responsibility.

Commitment to user involvement must be evident in policy and practice from top to bottom of the organisation. (Days of Change, 1998)

The conventional understanding of the phrase 'user involvement' is people collectively working together to express their views about services and influence changes. In the learning difficulties field this is usually through self-advocacy groups, day centre committees, representation on a wide range of professional or governmental working groups or involvement in other service-based initiatives, such as quality action groups or service monitoring groups.

Using this definition of user involvement has presented particular challenges during the past two years of the Changing Days work. We were focusing on people with complex disabilities and high support needs, people whose experience of life was mostly extremely limited, whose communication methods were often unconventional and who, in a number of instances, clearly did not want to be in group situations.

People with complex needs have the same right to have their voices heard as anyone else. Yet they are the ones so often left out of the now-familiar range of activities outlined above. The challenge for us has been to figure out different ways of including them. Are 'the usual ways' appropriate anyway?

If not, what is? How do we make sure that people with complex needs have a chance to influence services just as any other person who uses those services?

What did we know before we started?

We knew that we were venturing into relatively uncharted territory. Although there are some good practice examples to draw on, they are comparatively few. Many self-advocacy groups now do include people with additional disabilities, for instance making sure that there is access for wheelchair users or providing support for people who can't see or hear well. Could we build on this experience, working with local user groups in the sites to take the work further?

It seemed important, too, to keep focused on the essential Changing Days goals of increasing people's opportunities in the community and building friendships and connections in community places. The overall aim would not just be how people with complex needs could be integrated into user groups, but how user groups might work to make sure that the voices and views of their less able friends and colleagues were heard. This would involve acting as advocates and influencing services on their behalf.

How we worked

The three Changing Days development sites presented different starting points for addressing this challenge.

Harperbury Hospital

The disabilities of the people at Harperbury Hospital meant that it would be inappropriate, certainly in the short-term, to approach 'user involvement' in the usual 'group' ways. But individually the users were very capable of making known what they thought about their own lives and what they liked and disliked. In most cases, they needed help from a member of staff or relative to express their opinions. As their lives changed for the better, it can be said that their wishes were heard and acted upon. Also, because of the positive outcomes achieved during Changing Days for the group as a whole, the person-centred planning process is now being used to help all other residents in the hospital. So, we could say that their voices have indeed influenced the future direction of services.

All the people in the Changing Days group were due to move out of hospital to new homes in the community. We had plans to see whether there were any self-advocacy groups in the different areas they were going to with whom we might link up and work with. In the event, we did not have time to pursue this idea further than the very exploratory stages. Some people's plans for moving out changed or were delayed during the course of the project so we did not know where everyone was going or when. The people who did move out were fully occupied settling into their new homes and getting used to the new people immediately around them before any thought could be given to contacts further afield. For some people this could take many months or longer.

Newham and Knowsley

The situation in the other two sites was quite different. Both had keen and enthusiastic groups of users who were either already very actively involved in self-advocacy groups or who wished to be. There were no geographical complications as all the people with complex needs who would be the focus of the work were living in the local area. Both sites also had strong commitment and support from frontline staff and management.

In Newham, there is a well-established People First branch office that was already very involved in service development and monitoring. The Changing Days user group set up there consisted of representatives from local user groups and day centre committees, and was organised and led by People First staff.

Knowsley had previously had a service-based self-advocacy group but it had ceased functioning. However, there were a number of enthusiastic individuals keen to re-start the group, backed by equally enthusiastic and committed managers and staff. The advent of Changing Days provided the incentive and a user group was quickly established.

Aims of the user work

Initial meetings of the Newham and Knowsley user groups saw time being spent discussing what Changing Days was aiming to do, what was meant by people with complex needs and ideas for how they might be involved.

The overall aims of the work with user groups were to:

- show how staff and users can change services together
- help staff to listen
- make user groups stronger
- help people learn about new choices, e.g. college, office work, photography
- help people understand how their lives might change.

In addition, the following aims, specifically relating to people with complex needs, were agreed:

- to see how people who need a lot of support might be involved in checking services
- to see how the user group might directly help people with complex needs, e.g. by getting involved with one or more planning circles
- to make a book about places to go and things to do locally that are accessible and friendly towards people with learning difficulties, including people who need a lot of support.

By the end of the two years, the Newham and Knowsley groups had achieved a great deal in terms of what they could do themselves as a group, but it proved more difficult to make progress with aims that related directly to people with complex needs.

Achievements

With People First already established in Newham, there was a good base of experience in user involvement to build on. The group did particularly well in producing a book of locally accessible places to go and things to do. Members also helped with a survey of what people in day centres thought about their services.

As the Knowsley group were starting 'further back', they needed to spend more time learning to work together and on re-establishing their group. They made steady progress and have become the voice for people with learning difficulties in the area. Their achievements include running their own user conferences and speaking to the social services committee about what they wanted from day services. They have also started collecting information for a local directory.

What helped?

Enthusiasm of service users

It was clear that people enjoyed working together to express their ideas on current and future services, and on how they could be involved in the changes. They knew that they were listened to and would get support to turn their ideas into practical goals they could achieve themselves. We saw people grow in confidence and ability as the work progressed.

Management commitment

In both Newham and Knowsley, middle and senior managers provided financial support additional to 'usual' service costs (e.g. non-service venues for user conferences, refreshment costs for meetings). Extra funding enabled a local community user group to produce excellent pictorial minutes of meetings.

Managers also provided moral and verbal support through regular attendance at user group meetings and by making representations to 'higher authorities'.

Frontline staff commitment

In both sites there was a number of frontline staff who gave consistent and skilled hands-on support, which was essential in helping to achieve the groups' goals. They assisted in practical ways, keeping the groups on task and helping members learn new skills to be part of and operate a group.

What hindered?

Both Newham and Knowsley were going through a period of great change. So, in spite of the consistent commitment from many frontline staff, the lack of enough hands-on support did slow progress at times. Staff who were already involved wanted to do more, but were unable to because the many other changes going on within their services created extra stress and limits on time and resources.

Changes in staffing during the course of the project – both at managerial level and of people providing direct support – caused hiccups in planned action. This meant that, on occasions, the Changing Days objectives had to give way to other group priorities. Going at a pace that the service users can manage is an important principle of user involvement that needs to be taken on board, even if this means that some goals may not be achieved.

Sometimes progress was held up by what seemed to be a lack of communication between day services and residential services (for example, the need for people to have more support from staff in their homes to get to meetings). This may in fact have been the need for more co-ordination – or it might have been lack of staff or the need for a greater overall understanding in the service of the importance of user involvement. We did not have the time to develop this aspect.

Involving people with complex needs

We learned that the aim of involving people with complex needs, not surprisingly, will need more time than we had available during the project – taking into account also the stages of development of the groups and local circumstances.

The groups at Newham and Knowsley spent time thinking about the type of support needed for people with complex disabilities and how they might be involved in group work. Knowsley is working towards involving someone in their meetings. Newham got to the stage of planning an outing for a member of the group who uses a wheelchair, with the idea of using this as a 'pilot' project but, in the end, were unable to make further progress before the project ended.

The future

Both Newham and Knowsley were keen to develop ideas for involving people with complex needs, such as linking up with their planning circles, and it is to be hoped that they will get this opportunity as person-centred planning proceeds in their areas.

The reasons for the success or otherwise of various aspects of the work as outlined above will be familiar to readers, but they do serve to reinforce the importance of having user-involvement so embedded in the service's values and ways of working that it will survive the inevitable bureaucratic ups-and-downs of statutory services.

Chapter 11

New lifestyles – managing the changes

Today, managers face significant challenges to reshape public and voluntary sector day services for people who have complex disabilities. This is a difficult and demanding task, and managers leading the way need to embrace a range of skills and talents and to find ways in which they can regenerate not only their services but themselves. Managers will need to:

- think strategically
- envision with some clarity a better future
- inspire the trust of carers and those using services
- motivate all to participate in a complex change process
- be capable of excellent communication
- develop good leaders throughout the organisation, who represent users, carers, staff and ordinary citizens
- understand the cultural differences between a health and social care approach using the best characteristics to improve people's lives.

Establishing clear values

In order to work through successful change and improve people's lifestyles, it is vital that everyone signs up to the same set of values and principles. Developing a set of principles to promote the needs, rights and wishes of people with complex disabilities will revolve around beliefs that:

- people with complex disabilities are to be supported under the same principles of community inclusion as those who are more able

- needs can best be met within a collaborative and joint commissioning approach across health, social services, education and the benefits agency
- listening and responding to the needs, hopes and wishes of each man or woman with complex disabilities – including those who are non-verbal – through a person-centred planning process is essential to achieving individual goals
- service design and proposals should be based on the aggregation of these person-centred plans
- accountability of staff is to the person they are supporting, not solely to the organisation
- services should not be provided in segregated settings but alongside non-disabled citizens, such as in leisure centres and colleges.

Achieving consensus and ownership of these values at an early stage in the process of change will bring greater rewards for people with complex needs. A significant move away from congregate, collective settings towards individualised service provision is woven in to each of these service values and will influence how all key players across health, education, social services, housing, benefits and leisure services – as well as ordinary community members – will respond.

Strategic changes

Managing strategic change has proved extremely difficult in public sector services over the last decade. It has been all too easy for organisations to lose direction, become engrossed in organisational problems and cease to stay focused on individual need. They spend a great deal of time in discussion about internal difficulties, processes and policies rather than on positive changes for the individual. The real challenge for managers is to turn values and policy directives into improved quality lifestyles for one individual at a time. Managers are more likely to succeed in this area if they:

- focus energy on outcomes for individuals – not on organisational issues
- recognise the potential benefits of supported employment and develop opportunities for people with high levels of need
- jointly commission and provide services to encourage pooled funding, skill exchange and a common culture across health, social services and education and leisure departments
- foster a community development approach to build the capacity of communities and organisations to welcome and support people with complex disabilities in a range of ordinary settings
- use imagination and creativity to find opportunities for people with complex disabilities to contribute positively to their communities.

Working for the State Governor: an example from Madison, Wisconsin

Darwin spent 20 years in a long-stay hospital before moving to a home in the community. He has no spoken communication, uses a wheelchair and only has full use of his left arm and hand. Over time, much effort was put into understanding what Darwin wanted from life: he was keen to work. The local supported employment agency decided to try 'job carving' to find the right job for Darwin. Firstly, the agency did an analysis of his work skills and interests and then set out to find an appropriate workplace.

Thanks to the enthusiasm of the State Governor, the State Capitol building in Madison wished to offer employment to people who needed high levels of support. With Darwin in mind, the agency did an audit of jobs that matched Darwin's skills and a tailor-made job was 'carved' out. His tasks are mostly administrative. The employment agency provided him with an envelope-filling machine and equipment to align papers so they can be stapled properly. Darwin's workstation is near the Governor's office, where he is included as a member of the Governor's support staff.

Managing changes in service design and practice

While resistance to change is still a common reaction, more staff, parents and users are becoming allies for change – particularly in relation to individualising services. More people are insisting on individuals having a greater say on how funding is spent, e.g. closer control of their money and more choice over who supports them. There is a range of initiatives that managers can use to support this, including:

- access to Direct Payments for people with complex disabilities
- better use of the Independent Living Fund, creating more individual choice and involvement
- users choosing who supports them and interviewing support workers on a regular basis
- users and carers reviewing services and giving feedback to influence service change.

Within this new culture, managers will have to oversee the shift from service and staff-led services to increased user-driven and defined services. An obvious change is breaking down funding to provide individualised approaches. Commissioners will increasingly need to provide individual service agreements.

Moving from assessing need to understanding individuals

During the second phase of Changing Days, information gained from parents during the person-centred planning process showed that pooling knowledge in a three-way partnership between parents, users and staff was the most effective way of working (see Chapter 2).

In this way a partnership culture can be created, where pooling knowledge, agreeing goals, holding the person at the centre of the process and constantly striving for new opportunities and development are more easily achieved. This is a long way from a traditional care management assessment process.

Changes within the care management process are necessary if the best use is to be made of the skills of the limited number of care managers. In many areas, the care management system is seriously under-resourced, and hard-pressed care managers feel they do not have the time they need to do their job effectively. Enabling frontline support workers to be more formally involved in carrying out assessments is one possibility that should be explored.

Achieving holistic assessment is vital. The culture in health care settings, in particular, is not conducive to looking at social network building, relationship building and emotional needs. On the other hand, social care settings need to develop a much greater understanding of the importance of people's health care. One result of these differences is multiple systems of assessment, which result in duplication of effort and a waste of resources. A shared system of assessment across health, social services, education, housing, leisure and benefits agencies would not only be more efficient but really move things forward for a user-focused service.

Designing services to be user-driven requires skill, persistence and attention to detail. Moving away from dependence on buildings to community inclusion and taking advantage of new community opportunities will require changes in how people work and in the nature of their jobs. Redesigning the structure of a service in response to the aggregation of person-centred plans will result in services that empower individuals to make choices, to participate and to develop as individuals. New posts will need to be created, such as:

- job coaches
- staff with specialist skills to communicate with users who are non-verbal
- community link workers
- leisure and arts staff to negotiate opportunities in the community
- individual support workers (chosen by the person being supported)
- health support workers linking with GPs

- workers to support the development of circles of support and social network building.

M ichael is a young man with very severe autism, who used to be subject to extreme self-injurious behaviour up to 60 times an hour. It was very difficult to get to know him or understand what he wanted from life. Over time, and with sensitive 'listening' to what Michael seemed to want, it was agreed that he should have a home of his own, where he could live by himself with the one-to-one support that he needed.

The next step was to find Michael some meaningful occupation during the day. One thing he enjoyed and was good at was chopping up carrots and onions. So staff have built on this skill and he now has a job putting together salads, which are sold each day as part of a lunch service in his neighbourhood.

Managing change in a community

Acting as a catalyst to change the community's reactions to people who have complex disabilities is another important task on a manager's agenda. This includes:

- lobbying for a corporate approach to disability issues, shared across environmental services, health, education, leisure services and community groups
- including environmental changes in any strategic plan, e.g. not just entry ramps and accessible toilets but also suitable changing areas for disabled adults in public venues, and awareness and skills training for staff
- influencing NHS trust board members and local authority councillors to become leaders for change when being lobbied by concerned carers

- supporting GPs and primary health care staff to better understand and serve the unique needs of people with learning disabilities, particularly those with complex disabilities.

The Trowbridge Centre

Funding from a Single Regeneration Budget for the Trowbridge Estate in the London Borough of Hackney will be used to change the focus of the Trowbridge Centre, a conventional day centre for people with learning difficulties. It will become a community resource for all by:

- offering space for community groups and activities, which people with learning difficulties can also join
- working with the local community to identify their needs, responding to these by running small businesses, such as a café or photocopying service, which could provide employment opportunities.

Thus it aims to make people with learning difficulties better-off financially and also to find valued roles in a setting where they receive support while contributing to their local community.

Working in a collaborative culture across health, social services and education

To work collaboratively, leaders and managers need to understand the different cultural beliefs, values and practices that exist across different services. With regard to people with complex needs, a very significant opportunity is the exchange between health and social services of skills relating to health care needs and community and individual development. Managers will need to prioritise the range of health care issues that have emerged for people with complex learning disabilities over the last few years. In doing so there is a real opportunity to reduce the health inequalities so often experienced by this group. At the top of the agenda, managers will need to put in place efficient, effective services that will tackle:

- untreated, undiagnosed poor health
- problems with over-medication
- lack of contact with specialist health providers, such as neurologists, who have a special understanding of epilepsy
- problems with swallowing and aspiration of food which, if left untackled, can be life-threatening
- the national shortage of occupational therapists and speech and language therapists to support people with complex needs.

Staff development

Staff development strategies are a vital part of service redesign if managers are going to achieve a new type of service that will support individuals in their chosen lifestyle. For example, staff will need training and development in supporting people to initiate and sustain friendships and social networks. Other areas include:

- person-centred planning and facilitating circles of support
- moving from assessment to lifestyle planning, which emphasises the whole person and opportunities for community inclusion and citizenship
- training social care staff to understand health care needs
- developing the role of the learning disability nurse, including understanding of community development while retaining real expertise in health and health training for social care staff.

Managing partnerships with families

Partnership means developing a strategy which is grounded in active involvement, is on-going, has commitment from parents and professionals, has a framework or timetable which keeps the process on track and where everyone shares in the aims and can see the outcomes.[1]

The respite needs of parents and other family carers have been reasonably well met within a traditional day service model. The usual hours of 10 a.m.–4 p.m. have provided much needed opportunities for carers to pursue their own interests in leisure, employment and community involvement. As services move towards more individualised support and a less predictable timetable, carers, understandably, have been sceptical and concerned.

A person-centred planning process will need to come up with an agreement that meets all parties' needs. Carers who work full-time, for example, are likely to need more 'respite care' than one or two days a week. A range of initiatives will be needed, which might include developing leisure opportunities, increasing people's social activities with new friends or in drop-in clubs or centres, perhaps run by users themselves.

Over the years, many carers have lost faith in services to provide support that really understands the unique needs of the individual. Managing a process where carers reinvest in a relationship with services is a complex and potentially difficult situation. Parents and other family members hold a great deal of information about their child or relative, and their collaboration and involvement in creating a good person-centred plan is essential. Much work needs to be done to manage this process and ensure that parents also become leaders alongside managers of services.

A framework of quality

Managers will want to achieve quality and be clear about areas for priority. Suggested yardsticks are:

- people's needs are met through person-centred planning and the involvement of their wider social network or circle of support
- each person has an annual health care check, which the learning disability community nurse is accountable for implementing
- care managers roles are clear in maximising opportunities for individualised funding and in designing complex care packages
- service evaluations are carried out by users and carers and are fed into the redesign of services
- staff contracts are flexible so that staff work when users require them. This is to include evenings, late nights and weekends
- people who are non-verbal have a communication 'passport', Filofax or other aid suitable to their needs, which gives a clear explanation of support needs, likes and dislikes, non-verbal signs, etc.
- services should always be in inclusive settings and maximise opportunities for interaction with non-disabled members of the public
- new forms of funding, such as corporate sponsorship, European funding and Lottery bids, are found to increase opportunities and move away from total dependence on public sector finance
- small, nimble, person-centred organisations should be encouraged. They can be freed up from the constraints of the public sector and are capable of staying focused on one individual at a time
- reduce hierarchies within organisations. A flatter structure improves communication and promotes a more democratic environment.

Conclusion

Despite increased awareness about the needs of people with complex disabilities, many individuals remain caught in unimaginative routines, within hard-pressed public sector services. The challenge for services remains to create real changes in 'difficult-to-change' service systems. They will need to tackle the major step of redesigning and refocusing services and adapting the culture. Without these changes, organisations are unlikely to achieve the desired improvements in people's lives.

Reference

1. McIntosh B and Whittaker A, editors. *Days of Change.* London: King's Fund, 1998.

Chapter 12

Reflections from service managers

Change in Knowsley

Introduction

It was not difficult to 'sell' Changing Days to staff and managers in Knowsley. A culture of change was already well established. The Learning Disability Service had been challenged by a 'Passing' evaluation some years previously and much work had been undertaken to underpin services with values and principles that put the client first. Hostels had been closed down and clients relocated to ordinary houses within the borough, appropriately supported by a network of staff. The 'special needs' units had been disbanded and clients with complex needs were integrated within the whole service. This had both positive and negative effects. Positive in the sense that there were more opportunities for the clients to participate in everyday activities that other people enjoyed and in that they had some more able role models to whom they could relate. The negative side was the amount of individual time that staff were able to spend with them. In the special needs unit they had been the focus of staff attention, now they had to share time with other clients – many of whom were more able to express their wants and needs.

Staff were aware of this problem and felt that Changing Days, with its focus on people with complex needs, would enable them to start redressing the balance.

The shape of the project

There were two distinct strands to the work in Knowsley. The first was to identify 16 individuals with complex needs, and work with each of them to create an Essential Lifestyle Plan and set up a planning circle. The second was to work with a group of more able people and empower them to advocate for clients with more complex needs, and to take a lead role in evaluating and shaping services.

Towards the conclusion of the project, the Service Manager interviewed as many of the facilitators (keyworkers) as possible and held discussions with line managers to identify the main lessons learned, as well as views on the benefits and barriers to progress that had been experienced. What follows is a 'distilled' version of those conversations.

Lessons learned about setting up the project

1. No extra resources can be a positive message

Although staff and managers were enthusiastic about improving services, there was an underlying suspicion that this might be 'another management whim', a 'nine-day wonder' that would involve them in extra work for no long-term benefit. It is particularly difficult to counter this attitude when you cannot point to any additional resources to underpin the change in direction. People were being asked to work with individuals to identify Essential Lifestyle Plans and set up circles of support but there were no additional staff to help with this. Clients who were not part of the project still had to have their needs met. This became a management challenge to do more and better quality work with the same resources. As people succeeded it became a very positive experience. The lesson learned is that challenge is good for us: we can do more than we think we can with our current resources. Challenge stimulates creativity and brings out problem-solving ability. Apathy and routine are banished as staff and clients work together to make things happen.

2. Preparation time is essential

Looking back, it is obvious to us now that we did not do enough work on the initial preparation stage. Staff and managers complained that there was insufficient information and, for a while, they were unclear about objectives and goals. Because of the timescales, staff were not involved in selecting people to take part in the project. This resulted in some lack of ownership in the early stages.

In future, we will ensure that:

- all information is available, if possible in writing, so that managers understand the objectives, functions and desired outcomes of the project

- staff are identified and involved from the earliest possible point in the project and invited to be part of it rather then feeling that it has been imposed on them

- more information is given and more question and answer sessions are held before the project officially starts so that managers and staff can clarify their understanding of expectations.

What the staff learned

1. We learned much more about the social consequences of disability. The project helped us to focus on people's lifestyles and contrast them with our own

2. We had time to put principles into practice without distractions and were surprised at how much we discovered about individuals

3. Usually we work with small groups. The project enabled us to spend quality time with individuals and we found that identifying an Essential

Lifestyle Plan is all about the person, not just his/her perceived needs. It was like giving someone a personality on paper. It has made us want to work in this way with everyone

4. We learned much more quickly about what works and what doesn't because we were getting immediate feedback from interaction with the client and family

5. The key to getting family/carers to support the project was to establish an honest personal relationship with them and to make yourself accountable to them. If things go right you can celebrate together and that cements the relationship. If things go wrong the carers know a name and a face with whom they can discuss their problem. The key-worker will not try to 'pass the buck' to someone else

6. We were surprised at how much we learned about the client from carers. We realised that although the client may have been in the service for years, we had never had an in-depth discussion with the carer about their son or daughter's likes and dislikes, personal traits and habits – things that perhaps only they would know about. For years, one client used a 'sign' of pointing to his right ear. Staff were not too sure what he meant but had interpreted this as 'please listen to me'. At a circles meeting, the carer explained that it was the man's way of indicating he wanted a pencil because his father always had one tucked behind his right ear

7. We could make life easier for everyone if we had proper links and communication systems between agencies. For example, shared documentation between children and adults divisions within social services would greatly improve the transition process for 16 to 19-year-olds

8. We learned how good it feels to be part of a national project. You can feel isolated and have no idea whether your practice is good or bad compared to other parts of the country. Changing Days gave us the opportunity to be part of something bigger and to get a 'feel' for what we are doing well and where we can still improve

9. We felt guilt at times for being given quality time to do this work whilst we could see colleagues struggling

10. We have become bolder in asking for things that cost money! Previously we did not ask for things that required financial resources. The project has taken us to a new level where we do ask. It can be both rewarding and frustrating but it is always a good learning experience

11. It taught us to be creative and not to expect that one method or solution would work for everybody. Some people liked their circle meeting to be formal, others preferred informality. There isn't one 'right' way. We can negotiate with people to find out what's best for them. Circles create a more equal opportunity between staff, clients and carers

12. You must have support from the top. If the manager doesn't allow you the time to work in this way and doesn't value the work, then it won't happen

What members of the 'Taking Control' user group learned

1. We can do a lot more than people think if given the right opportunities and support

2. We were amazed that we were able to give presentations at a local authority council meeting and at a health authority meeting. This was the first time service users in our area had done this. People liked our presentations, and said they had learned a lot from them

3. A member of our group helped to chair the Changing Days national conference for service users

4. Sometimes it is difficult to get other service users involved: they don't seem to care. We need to make our group so interesting that if our meeting times clash with other activities, people will choose to come to our meetings

How services will change as a result of Changing Days phase 2

1. We will roll out a phased programme of Essential Lifestyle/Person-centred Plans for all clients

2. We have obtained one year's funding to employ a Circles Co-ordinator who will support staff in setting up circles with clients

3. We will consult clients and carers first and in more depth

4. We will involve the 'Taking Control Group' in advocacy, planning and evaluating services. They are already involved in interview panels when we recruit staff but we will now extend the training to include any client who wishes to be involved

5. We will concentrate on giving an individualised service to clients wherever possible, recognising that this results in personal development for the individual, a better quality of life and more job satisfaction for staff

6. We will try to maintain national links with other learning difficulties services, to widen our perspective and exchange knowledge of good practice

7. We will challenge our own practices, recognising that services delivered in the community can still be 'institutional' in nature

8. We have learned to ask clients first, not last, in any consultation process and we recognise that our clients are the people from whom we can best learn

Change at Harperbury Hospital

Introduction

Harperbury Hospital, Horizon NHS Trust is in the final stages of closure, with its last long-term service due to close in December 2000. The aim of Horizon's project was to see how people with severe learning disabilities still living in hospital could be offered the same range of daytime opportunities as those people already in the community. Through the person-centred planning process, the aim was to make sure that when these people moved out of hospital, they would be able to continue and develop a lifestyle of their choice, based on each person's individual wishes and needs. This would require working across organisational boundaries, the support of community providers and high levels of commitment and motivation from those already caring for individuals within Horizon.

Background

Fifteen people were chosen to take part in the project. Only three had relatives who were in regular contact; one other person had a brother who asked to be kept informed but could not play an active role due to his age (78) and state of health. Sadly, one person died during the course of the project. Another was removed following pressure from parents. The average age of the 13 remaining residents was 53 years.

Lessons learned

The aim was to set up a planning circle around each individual and use the person-centred planning process to develop a life plan. The first step was to identify people who would act as facilitators for the planning circles. They were mostly named nurses. Then events were organised, which brought together key people who could support the residents to achieve changes in their lives. Very soon, issues began to emerge that affected the process of person-centred planning. Many named nurses had only recently moved from units that had closed and did not know their residents very well, and so where residents relied completely on their named nurse for supplying information to their planning circle, it was difficult to build up a picture of the person. It soon became evident, too, that individuals' records were heavily biased towards medical information: knowledge of residents in a social context was at best patchy.

The involvement of parents had both positive and negative outcomes. The most negative resulted in parents removing their child from the project. Where active participation occurred, the parents' involvement had a direct and positive affect on resettlement plans for their son:

David's mother and father were very sceptical to begin with but by the end of the planning circle day had changed their views. They felt they had been listened to and they appreciated the time spent talking about their son as a person rather than as a set of medical problems.

The information they shared in the planning circle was invaluable. For example, they explained how he uses different coloured pens to indicate different needs – something that even staff who had worked with him for many years did not know.

David was due for resettlement and people from the home chosen for him also came to the planning circle day. As a consequence of getting to know more about David on that day, they realised that this placement was probably not right for him. This was very important because David had already experienced one failed resettlement. David now has a new home in the community that can better meet his needs.

The project has clearly demonstrated that person-centred plans created in partnership with new providers before a person moves out stand a far greater chance of being maintained and built upon after the person has gone to live in their new home.

The project has also shown the need to spend time researching and recording the 'social' and family aspects of each person's life history. This is particularly important for people who have no contact with relatives. It is also very important given the many changes of named nurses a service user may have during the process of closure. Because of this, at Harperbury it was decided that the role of facilitator was better met by day service staff who could maintain greater continuity.

After people moved out, the geographical distance between the Trust and new providers has made it difficult to maintain influence and motivation. It largely depends on the enthusiasm and commitment of the provider. Where this has been achieved, individuals have made progress in achieving their agreed goals.

Charlie had been living in Horizon NHS Trust for over 20 years. Soon after he was admitted, contact with his mother was lost. As a result of the person-centred planning his most important goal was to re-establish contact with his mother.

With support from his social worker and the enthusiasm of Charlie's new care staff, Charlie and his mother met again at a birthday meal. Work has now begun to re-establish contact with his sister. Charlie's 'circle of support' has begun to grow.

Bringing influence to bear, however positive, on some community agencies requires careful and considered diplomacy. The Trust's 'best efforts' can be perceived as an inability to 'let go' of a service user once they have been formally discharged. With this in mind, transferring ownership of a genuine person-centred model has proved difficult when trying to avoid sounding self-righteous.

The bigger picture

The Changing Days work has had a profound impact on service design within the Trust, which has been beneficial at a time when Horizon is undergoing radical change. The philosophy of social inclusion is now an important part of new operational policies, advocating person-centred planning as a practical tool for achieving greater empowerment for people with learning difficulties.

Important lessons were learned about how the Trust records a person's life. Taking time to reflect on past practices highlighted the need to provide a more holistic picture, including social as well as medical information.

Training has been devised to ensure that staff consider service users' needs and wishes within a wider social context. One practical way of doing this has been to guide staff in creating 'life diaries.' The 'life diary' is then used as a basis of personalised information from which to proceed with the development of a planning circle and as a means to start looking at the real – rather than assumed – needs of the person with whom staff are working.

Hertfordshire Social Services is currently undergoing a review of its day services and staff from Horizon were invited to participate. This model of person-centred planning has proved useful in starting to bridge organisational gaps and work in closer partnership.

Oakland College, the local education provider, has also seen the value of this way of working and has enthusiastically sought to play an active role alongside Horizon in making the person-centred planning process an effective tool for achieving a better quality of life for residents.

Participating in the Changing Days project has provided a foundation on which to build positive change that will have long-term impact on the approach used by the Trust to deliver services to people with severe and complex learning disabilities. However, this cannot be achieved by working in isolation. In this instance, experience has shown that organisations do seem to be more prepared to work across professional boundaries to create varied lifestyles for individuals.

Chapter 13

Collecting the evidence – measuring progress

During the course of the Changing Days work, there were numerous stories of positive changes in the lives of individuals. However, in order to gain a more comprehensive assessment of the changes, a method of collecting comparative information was built in from the beginning. The aim was to produce an overall before-and-after picture of the changes in people's lives during the course of the project.

Each of the three sites taking part agreed to choose up to 15 people with complex needs to take part in the initiative. In total, 39 people were chosen and 32 remained involved to the end of the project. Baseline information and an overview of each person's current quality of life were gained through a person-centred plan undertaken by a planning circle led by the individual. The picture of quality of life was taken again at the end of the project.

Seventy per cent of the group's participants used non-verbal communication. Half had a physical disability and used a wheelchair or needed special equipment. They ranged in age from 19 to 59 years.

What did people see as a positive future?

During the first few months, person-centred plans were completed for each individual and a picture was built up of their hopes and dreams for the future. These included:

- the chance to have a job and the support to do that job

- to have more friends and acquaintances
- to have a boyfriend or girlfriend
- to have more choice in daily living activities
- to go out in the evenings and at weekends
- to take part in activities that were relaxing and rewarding
- to take part in sports and enjoy music and art
- to go on holiday
- to do something adventurous
- to be more independent, particularly of parents and family
- to have a home of one's own
- to be able to travel.

The impact of person-centred planning and better day opportunities

The most significant gain for people was higher self-esteem and a more positive belief in themselves and their potential. This was seen in 80 per cent of the group. Almost three-quarters were seen to be more assertive and/or more sociable. Several people felt enabled to make more decisions.

One man felt confident enough to make choices concerning how he spent his money and, in doing so, learned lessons about budgeting. He decided to buy a dog but found that he couldn't look after it and also that it was expensive. He also bought a mobile phone, but realised it was too costly after several months of paying expensive bills.

Nine people reduced their attendance at the day centre. Substitute activities included voluntary work, going to a clubhouse, joining the Rambler's Association and work experience. There was a small rise in the number of people who increased their involvement in further education – from four at the beginning of the project to seven at the end.

Supported employment

When the programme began in 1997, no one had work experience as part of their weekly routine. At the end of the project, five people were involved in some form of paid or unpaid employment.

While some real strides were made in helping people find and participate in employment, it still remained a minority that achieved this goal. A significant shift in resources is required to help larger numbers of people with complex needs succeed in the world of employment. Much skill, training and development work is needed to alter services so that they can better support people individually into employment.

Choices at home and relationships

A small number of people became more involved in activities within their own homes. Five individuals were seen to be contributing more to daily routines and to making choices at home. A small number of people increased relationships and friendships with people outside of service systems. At the beginning of the work three people had outside relationships; when the work ended five people had experienced or were experiencing outside relationships.

In the area of communication, there were a number of interesting comments made by family or staff members. One young woman was seen to have higher expectations in life and was expressing her wishes much more actively. One support worker commented that, 'She now says what she is feeling, not just what she is thinking.' Another individual valued himself more, as seen by the support worker, and several people were felt to be more contented, more relaxed and more at ease with themselves. Overall, seven people were seen to have improved in their communication style, making their needs and wants better known to their families, friends and carers.

While everyone participating expressed wishes to do a variety of things, one of the real problems lay in accessing support staff who could be freed up to support one person at a time. The old historical approaches to providing day care in congregate settings militated against individualising people's day activities. As a result, there was still a heavy reliance at the end of the project on day centres for people with complex needs.

Leisure and community involvement

The number of individuals taking part in leisure activities more than doubled – from seven to 15. Everyone participated in ordinary settings alongside non-disabled citizens.

Twelve individuals increased their involvement in their local community. Unpaid friends, family and advocates supported several, while a small number received paid individualised support because of a redesign of the way staffing was offered. In the long-term, it is hoped that people who joined clubs, for example a young man who joined the Everton Football Supporters Club in Liverpool, will secure hands-on help from their peers within the clubs. It may be that this takes some time to establish and the picture will be more positive in a few years time. Community activities also included going to concerts, joining a church, going to nightclubs. Only one person decreased their involvement in the community.

Transition

People coming from school and entering the day service seemed more flexible and willing to try new things, to take risks and to resist the idea of attending the day centre five days a week. We know from our experience in the UK and in the USA that helping people in transition to make choices about their adult lifestyle is important in opening up new opportunities.

Achieving a picture of health

In order to be able to participate in jobs, leisure and education, people need to be fit and healthy. Our work confirmed that people with complex needs are often not well served in this regard.

All the participants in the Changing Days project had a health care check at the beginning of their involvement in the project. This revealed a high level of undiagnosed or untreated health problems. Some GPs struggled to assess even their basic health care needs, for example finding it difficult to weigh individuals because they were in wheelchairs, to test their sight because they were partially sighted or, generally, because of people's high level of disability and emotional distress during a physical examination. Some of the key health problems highlighted included:

- high levels of undiagnosed ill health such as thyroid disease, diabetes and hypertension
- a high number of people on long-term medication, with repeat prescriptions, not having been seen by their GP
- a number of young people with complex health care problems in their early 20s remaining under the care of paediatricians for a lack of any appropriate adult physician
- difficulties with food aspiration, swallowing problems and a tendency to be recommended for tube feeding if the swallowing and aspiration difficulties persisted.

People who couldn't speak up for themselves were at a much higher level of risk from poor health and undiagnosed diseases. Annual health care checks, although recommended by the Royal College of General Practitioners, had clearly not been carried out and some GPs requested financial remuneration to complete the health checks. In social care settings, social care staff lacked knowledge and understanding to pick up early signs and symptoms that would lead to the person going to the GP. Staff development and training is required to help social care staff understand the health care requirements of people with complex needs.

In some cases, learning disability nurses were accountable for the health of the individual and helped to inform and train frontline social care staff. This type of accountability structure seems to improve health and set out clear lines of responsibility. As more people move into social care settings, this issue needs to be tackled.

Conclusion

While by no means as comprehensive or as detailed as we would have liked, the above serves to demonstrate some of the challenges in changing services for people with complex needs. It is relatively straightforward to achieve positive changes for individuals in their daily lives in the short term. Achieving our ultimate goal of full inclusion for everyone – including greatly increased employment opportunities – will require longer-term effort and commitment.

Chapter 14

Care management and planning circles

For a time it seemed that care management might be the answer: give care managers the budget, and they would decide what to buy for individuals. This would become a finance-led way to change what people got. But these projects and innovations have worked only for a few. (Days of Change, 1998)

A major challenge for services is how to provide an effective service based on supporting people's individual needs that also ensures financial accountability and makes appropriate use of prioritising within limited resources. On the face of it, care management would seem to have an important role to play here. To date, however, it has not proved as effective a tool as had been hoped. This chapter looks at the current situation with regard to care management, how it might fit into the person-centred planning process and how planning circles might have a role in supporting and contributing to the care management function.

Functions of a care manager

The care manager's role is to:

- assess a person's individual needs and take serious account of his/her wishes and preferences
- keep the planning process as person-centred as possible
- identify and commission other people who should be involved in order to make a comprehensive assessment
- identify and record needs that are statutory and needs that are recognised as good practice

- identify the best way of matching the individual's needs and preferences
- find providers who can deliver the services in a way that is qualitatively and financially best value, taking into consideration the budget and resources
- co-ordinate provision of the agreed services.

The current scene

The reality for most areas is that care management services are hard-pressed and under-resourced. Many service staff feel that they are offering a 'fire-fighting service', dealing only with those people most in crisis or perhaps those whose carers are making the loudest demands.

In spite of this, the majority of authorities do not appear to be strengthening the role or number of care managers. On the contrary, they are reducing the service or simply maintaining the number they need to cover their statutory responsibilities. Most care managers are very concerned about the future and some foresee their role becoming purely administrative.

Virtually all care managers say that they do not have the time they need to work creatively with service users. They can spend a high proportion of their time working with a small number of clients who require or demand a high level of input. These are often people with very mild learning difficulties, who might be at risk in the community or a risk to the community and who, in any case, may challenge the appropriateness of their needs being met by the learning difficulties sector.

The co-ordinating role of care managers is very time-consuming. As the number and variety of providers increase, the more demands are made of care managers to ensure arrangements are running smoothly, resolve difficulties and deal with increased bureaucracy.

While it is positive that more carers and service users are taking advantage of complaints procedures, a negative effect is that more and more time is spent responding to those who are able to make complaints – not necessarily those who have the greatest need. The care manager also needs to juggle the changing and possibly increasing needs of the service user and ever increasing demands on a limited budget.

As care plans become more complex, care managers are under pressure to dot every 'i' and cross every 't' to protect against complaints and litigation.

A 'culture of meetings' means that care managers spend a great deal of time simply trying to organise meetings, especially large planning meetings – not a good use of their time. Also, these meetings often do not include or empower the service user.

Targets and priorities

With increasing emphasis on reaching targets, care managers are often expected to ensure that certain numbers of assessments and reviews are carried out. This is at best an arbitrary way of monitoring the quality of the work that care managers are able or would wish to carry out. It is also about the ever-increasing business approach to 'people-centred' services.

Since care managers have to consider immediate budget implications, it is more difficult to argue for a care plan that may be costly initially but that could provide the input necessary to enable a person to become less dependent on services in the longer-term.

A growing trend towards setting ceilings on expenditure means that 'second-best' choices may be made on care plans. For example, if an individual supported living package that would meet a person's needs best is more expensive than a group residential placement, there will be an expectation to take the latter option.

Care management and planning circles

The following are thoughts that have emerged from working with planning circles. We do not presume to have definitive answers or solutions but pose these thoughts and questions for further consideration and discussion.

Can/should planning circles be part of the formal planning mechanism?

Care managers should be the hub of organising the planning, reviewing and costing of services for individuals. However, there are enormous pressures on managers' time. Planning circles are more likely to be able to spend the time necessary to really identify a person's needs and wishes, consider longer-term goals and be involved in more detailed planning of packages of care.

Circles could be assisted with detailed planning by the facilitator, a financial broker or other advisers that the circles could tap into. The circle would need to be trusted to produce information that the care manager could rely on. This would also avoid much duplication of effort.

A planning circle provides a very different atmosphere from the typical 'services' meeting. Keeping the relaxed and focused nature of the circle is a vital part of its success and it is essential that it is not hijacked by service output related professional involvement.

All assessments have to be evidence-based and, as far as possible, should be 'self-assessed' and owned by the person. Circles are more likely to have the time to be creative about how they help the person to state his/her needs and wishes and how they produce the person's lifeplan, e.g. using symbols, pictures, video, photographs, multimedia, etc.

There would need to be a clearly understood process by which the person's needs, wishes and desired goals are identified and taken up by the care manager and the commissioning agency.

Should care managers be part of the circle?

Care managers would benefit from getting a person-centred view of an individual's life/wishes/needs. The increased contact would help a care manager maintain a sense of the person and their individuality. They would also be gaining first-hand information on which to base clear, equitable decisions.

The circle may benefit from having the co-ordinator of the package present – the person who holds the budget. However, their presence may also have the effect of inhibiting the circle, preventing it from focusing on the person's needs, and sway it towards service needs in the form of the care manager's priorities and budget.

Although all staff have a duty of care, it is usually the care manager who is the person paid to protect the individual. So, who monitors circles? Who checks out the membership? Who decides the 'quality' of the outcomes? If anything goes wrong who will be held responsible?

Without a considerable increase in the number of care managers, it will not be possible to involve them as regular members of circles anyway.

Organisational issues

The joining of health and social service budgets may produce different priorities in the future. It may mean the reduction of duplication of efforts and better concentration of resources on individuals. There need to be clear philosophies and procedures to ensure that the desired outcomes and ways of working are person-centred.

The challenge is to make the process more flexible, so that money can be directed at the individual. But to what extent could care managers be involved? Perhaps the push here does need to come from facilitators and circles themselves, with advice from care management or someone with skills in individual finance? Currently, much money is tied into in-house services and block contracts. If money could be used more individually, could circles become budget-holders? Care managers might become more like service brokers for those with circles, leaving them free to concentrate on people at risk and without support.

Does the local authority care manager have to be the only person who can undertake the 'care manager' role? This current requirement is mainly the result of the need to control the budget and cover statutory responsibilities. It may be possible to be more creative and flexible about who can be the designated care manager.

Moving forward

These issues need to be addressed at service level, with clear agreements about relative responsibilities and protocols. Such procedures should not be cumbersome and used as barriers to hide behind, but should provide a positive framework within which people can fulfil their roles to the benefit of the individual.

Chapter 15

Finance

New-style day services require radical new thinking about financial systems, costing and allocating resources.

The role of statutory services will look very different and will revolve around three activities – person-centred planning, personal support and community bridge building. This will require major change in the way finance is organised and used.

There is no magic financial formula to help us move from the present system to a new service. The challenge is to find such a radically new approach that financial modelling as it is today becomes a fiscal museum piece. (Days of Change, 1998)

Introduction

The anticipated higher cost of changing services and patterns of delivery is often the first consideration of service managers. It is assumed that individualised packages or using person-centred approaches will cost more, that moving away from group provision means solely one-to-one support. Often overlooked is the fact that ideal individualised support would target paid support where it is most needed. The effect of the support should be that people become increasingly linked into ordinary opportunities, gaining support as needed from those around them. A person would take part in activities, go to work and socialise with friends and colleagues rather than always with support workers, with obvious benefits to the individual in terms of self-esteem and a more ordinary lifestyle.

This chapter is based on the experience of the three development sites. It looks at the financial implications of trying to plan and provide people's day support and the financial issues involved in using planning circles compared to receiving all support through traditional day services.

Wider costs are also considered, such as use of other services, the cost of not using community resources and the costs of ill health.

The current position

In 1996, hospital and community health service expenditure on learning difficulties was £1372 million (5 per cent of total). Personal social services expenditure was £1080 million (13 per cent of total).[1]

There is very little clear financial information or research on providing specific types of support and no readily available information to give comparative costs of offering traditional services and more individualised community-focused supports. Costs are complicated, as there are often different agencies involved in supporting a person. Financial information may not be readily available as some of the support people receive may be from organisations funded or part-funded through, for example, European monies or voluntary donations.

Very little accurate information exists that can give a fair reflection of how finances relate to outcomes for people. Current ways of costing services vary from area to area and across different providers. Margaret Flynn highlighted this in 1994:[2]

- *In general, ways of costing services are very crude*
- *Public finances are only half the story*
- *Little progress has been made towards costing information on an individual basis. All existing cost information routinely published by health and social services is costed on an average basis – dividing the total cost by the number of service users*
- *It is difficult to identify all costs of a particular service as the number of different elements are often put together by a number of agencies, each with different accounting methods*
- *Costings which take a short-term perspective produce different conclusions from those which take long-term perspectives*

VIA raised further issues in 1998,[3] in terms of use of budgets not relating to people's needs or wishes:

- *Often the services being paid for are not what people with learning difficulties want or what they need*
- *When local authorities and health authorities buy support for people in their own homes, it does not cost as much money. People are happier in their own homes*

Many purchasers have little faith in the quality and competency of local provision. This makes the purchase of residential and institutional options more likely and casts doubts over the development of supported living. The development of accomplished local provision often results in good quality support in people's own homes.

There are 'opportunity costs' associated with failure to invest in people, relationships, skills and networks which might provide more meaningful and cost-effective arrangements for future generations of people with learning difficulties.

The financial situation for people with learning difficulties

In addition to this, people with learning difficulties are often poor, making access to ordinary living opportunities even more difficult:

They are persistently poor and are heavily dependent on low levels of benefits. Holidays, outings, new clothing, leisure and sport, feeding the cat, cannot be afforded without money from another source.

New clothing, access to public transport, having a pet, pursuing leisure and sporting interests are not sustainable on benefit income alone. People's families and service networks take the lead in making these items and opportunities available. An absence of these networks means that opportunities for 'normal' lives are severely curtailed.

In contrast with most adults in our society, people with learning difficulties produce little wealth and they make little use of banks and building societies. Their access to and management of their income is highly circumscribed.[4]

New ways of financial planning

To overcome the barriers and make planning more meaningful, we need new ways of costing support and measuring the benefits to people with learning difficulties and their carers.

We need a long-term view of the financial situation to be able to make a full cost benefit analysis of care packages and services. This may mean care managers or service providers learning new ways of projecting care needs and associated costs. An expensive package would be expected to reduce over time. Outcomes at reviews could be measured against this. Taking a short-term view mitigates against making an initial investment that may ultimately result in people having an improved quality of life, being more included in their communities and less dependent on services.

Most local authorities take a very short-term and discrete view of costs. This view is also very fragmented, for example John attends a day centre but has difficulty at home due to lack of adaptations. These adaptations could be funded by housing if he lived in local authority accommodation – at a cost of £3000 – but because he doesn't, it falls outside the criteria and social services continue paying £5000 per year to fund support for bathing.

There is also the benefits v. earned income argument: if someone is poor and living on benefits, they may 'cost' more in housing and other supports. If they had a job, they could gain money, use local resources. Day centres tend not to contribute to the local economy, but if a person is using ordinary community facilities, they will be using local cafés, paying to go to a swimming club, etc.

Central government and most local authorities have policies to combat social exclusion, reduce poverty and discrimination. They seek to promote the involvement of all in the life of the community and encourage economic activity of those previously seen as outside the job market. With 93 per cent of people with learning difficulties effectively unemployed, this will not happen without input. We need to find ways of securing the initial investment or ensuring that these costs are shared across departments, companies, and to be able to take a long-term view.

Costs are usually considered within each financial year, with the pressure being on social workers and budget managers to reduce costs. If they were able to take, say, a five- or ten-year view, a calculation could be made on average costs allowing for more realistic financial planning. Voluntary organisations are more geared up to flexible financial planning as they are more able to roll money into the next financial year.

If support costs within a package were seen as investment monies, expectations of outcomes could look very different, and a very different emphasis would be on service providers to link people into ordinary situations and friendships or to support people's existing friends and family members to involve them in a wider range of activities.

Only an holistic and long-term view of finances will allow us to meaningfully invest in the lives of people with learning difficulties.

Options for sharing financial responsibility

- Bridge building money could come from education, housing, leisure, Training and Enterprise Councils (TECS) or businesses

- Dovetailing with supported employment services
- Combine resources of residential, day, care management and health
- People's access to their own money needs to be addressed, and staff and others supported in tackling this issue with carers

---

Making sense of resources – action for managers

- Be aware of the organisation or council's strategy on social exclusion. Ensure people with learning difficulties are included in these policies. Get them, as an organisation, to commit finances
- Encourage the use of Independent Living Fund (ILF) and Direct Payments – this is not ideal, but it will have more of an impact
- Ensure that people are maximising their income through benefits
- Invest in supported employment services
- Work with organisations to help them implement the Disability Discrimination Act 1995, e.g. support the training of leisure staff, involve people with learning difficulties in consultation on things such as environmental services
- Make learning difficulties a mainstream area – ensure housing, education and environmental services are clear how their services can be accessed and are relevant to people with learning difficulties
- Nurture those organisations that support PCPs
- Ensure that standards are built into specifications for residential and supported living services that support and use PCPs
- Ensure that all staff are aware of the aims of inclusion
- Avoid parallel planning systems and duplication of roles

Financial considerations when developing planning circles

- Do we need to start small (e.g. because our staff skill base is low)? Or can we think bigger (e.g. because the service has received, say, a European grant)?
- Might it be possible to translate day service worker costs into individual money to spend on goals (e.g. one day service worker post at £20,000 could equate to £500 each for 40 people)?
- Paid facilitators at £20 per hour may be a more effective use of resources (i.e. time and generating new opportunities) than using existing day service staff

- Look at where money is currently being wasted – overlaps, duplicate assessments, lack of sharing of information
- Keep investing in contact with carers
- Look carefully at care packages that cost the most: are they really delivering what the person wants and needs? A planning circle may prove more cost-effective
- Build planning circles into specifications for day and residential services
- Avoid duplication of planning mechanisms, e.g. having a day service review, care management review and planning circle meeting for one individual

Using planning circles – the likely financial scenario

The immediate view

We are likely to see an immediate increase in real or equivalent costs. Staff members may be removed from their usual duties to facilitate the circle. The facilitators will need support and training. Other paid staff may be involved. Once the circle starts meeting and planning, needs and desires will be highlighted and expectations, rightly so, will rise. The group will take on an advocacy role. This may result in more demands for services, more one-to-one time or more resources and money to access opportunities.

The long-term view

Supported employment is a good example of the benefit of taking a long-term view. Much individual investment is needed to enable someone to gain and sustain a job. However, once working, the person's support needs decrease, associated support costs fall and the person is no longer dependent on traditional day services. (See Chapter 11 of *Days of Change.*)

Over time, the cost of supporting someone should decrease as they become more involved with ordinary community members. Society also benefits as people use ordinary facilities, thus contributing to the local economy, and become more active in the life of the community in general.

The moral view

Even if an increase in overall costs is predicted, perhaps it is right to support this model as a way of ensuring that people are meaningfully involved in planning their own futures and have the same opportunities in life as other members of society.

Costs and benefits involved in planning circles

Direct costs

- Staff training
- Facilitator time
- Staff time or replacement time
- Support time
- Facilitator support
- Infrastructure – buildings, management, supervision, etc.
- Room hire
- Costs of anyone involved as part of their job
- Costs for activities

'Hidden cost' benefits

- 'Free' time and out-of-hours time given by carers and others involved in the circles
- Meetings taking place in the person's own home
- Time given by any unpaid people in the circle
- Extra things that the person does that do not require a paid worker
- Any decreased use of existing services

Gains for the community

- Inclusion
- People may become economically active (over 93 per cent of people with learning difficulties are unemployed)
- People become consumers

- People use community resources – libraries, leisure centres
- People become contributing members of society
- Generally, people are healthier if they are more productive (higher rates of ill health and depression are recorded in unemployed people)

Additional benefits

- Improved communication between families, staff and others involved with the person
- Better relationship between service and carers
- Improved quality of life for the person
- The person is healthier
- More appropriate day service
- Free time from circle members
- Time saved re other meetings
- Involvement of other professionals who can gain accurate information more quickly

Is finance a barrier to participation in new activities?

Having money to take part in community activities, for example entry fees, trips to the cinema, did not appear to be an issue in the Changing Days projects. In Newham, the day service teams had money to subsidise 50 per cent of activity costs. This may be fine if talking about only a few people but may have other implications if extended over a whole service.

However, this money can also be considered an 'investment' in the future. It provides a useful way of introducing people to a range of activities that they could later fund themselves.

The planning circles were good at accessing resources, for example finding out about taxi cards or free bus services.

For nearly all the people living with carers, their personal money was absorbed into the family income, so it was usually the parents who agreed that money could be available for activities. People living in residential homes, supported living accommodation or in hospital usually had enough money to do most of the things identified within their circle, such as going to the theatre, horse riding, going out for a meal. Finances only became a potential barrier when considering things like holidays – especially if this meant the person also needing to meet some of the support costs.

The main barrier to doing things was considered to be the amount of finance available to pay support staff.

No one was in receipt of Direct Payments, and very few facilitators knew whether people were receiving money from the Independent Living Fund (ILF). There were only two examples of people receiving ILF, this being for respite care. The need for staff training in both ILF and Direct Payments was brought up as an issue in Newham.

Costs of support staff

The majority of facilitators were from day services (38 circles), five were from residential services and two from health trust services – a psychologist and an occupational therapist.

Costs associated with staffing did not come out as a discrete cost. Freeing up staff to support activities and attend circle meetings was mainly absorbed by the day services. There are examples also of residential homes that re-organised rotas to free up staff. Again, this may have been easier to absorb for a smaller number of service users than it would be for the majority. Staff were given time off in lieu for attendance at evening meetings. It was not uncommon for staff to get back time-and-a-half in lieu if the circle had met at a weekend or after 8 p.m.

There was an associated cost of providing replacement staff but, again, it did not add to the overall budget for the service. By and large, the involvement of support staff in planning circles was accommodated within existing resources by adjusting rotas, with other staff working with more people.

With regard to staff supporting circles, there could ultimately be a real saving in staff time because of the decrease in time spent, for example, linking with parents, going to meetings or attending reviews.

The main reason given for not being able to progress more quickly was the lack of available paid support. Many people said they could achieve more if more one-to-one time was available.

In both Knowsley and Newham, staff were freed up to offer one-to-one support on a regular basis. The time they spent on this varied from one day per week to one day per month. The time commitment from facilitators ranged from approximately 45 to over 200 paid hours per year. A minority of workers also supported the person in their own time. Several mentioned doing paperwork in their own time and not claiming for this.

Expenses for support workers

All facilitators talked about the service reimbursing their expenses, e.g. for bus fares, theatre trips, etc. One facilitator talked about funding herself when supporting the person to go out to the theatre as she had done this in her own time.

Expenses for other planning circle members

There were no examples of services or circles funding expenses for other members of the planning circles. Planning circle members paid their own expenses.

Costs associated with the overall process

Management time was largely absorbed within existing workloads. However, in changing services, support of the planning circles and introducing the approach, the sites had some extra overall resources or funding.

For all the sites, there was time input from Changing Days project workers in terms of support, advice and staff training. Changing Days funded the involvement of Acting Up to develop multimedia profiles with some people (see 'The moving-on picture – multimedia profiling', in Chapter 3).

In Newham, joint finance was secured to promote community building. This amounts to £120,000 over three years. It has so far paid for consultancy, support of the planning circles on a sessional basis and training for staff as part of the overall change process. It will also pay for a community builder post whose role will be to support circles, develop and extend the approach and build capacity in local organisations for them to become more inclusive. Further grant money is being obtained to fund a planning circle facilitator post.

New Initiatives (DoH) money in Knowsley will fund a circles co-ordinator post.

Horizon Trust obtained £3000 for staff training in 'Life Diaries'.

There was a big investment in all sites in terms of management time, staff time and training. There was in all cases a knock-on effect with the rest of the service having to absorb lower staff ratios at times.

Gains for the sites – including financial benefits and benefits in kind

Engaging other professionals

All areas did well in involving professionals from other service areas, e.g. colleagues from leisure services, health visitors, social services. This arose from the need to develop action goals and clear ways forward for the planning circles. The potential cost of doing this could have been massive, but sites were able to engage people who gave their time willingly.

Employment

The planning circles seemed more likely to consider employment an immediate or long-term possibility for the person than more service-focused reviews. Pursuing this would create different patterns of provision and costing in the long-term. This was seen as encouraging, given that employment is often not considered for people with more complex needs.

Accessing additional funding and resources

Having clear objectives to work towards gave the sites a focus for attracting some extra funding. Newham accessed £120,000 from Joint Finance to promote community building, Horizon accessed £3000 from Herts Consortium for education and staff development, and Knowsley accessed money to fund a new circles co-ordinator post.

Staff skills and approaches

Investment in the skill base of the staff team will have knock-on effects as they plan more creatively with other people who are looking for more community solutions. However, looking for different roles and skills for staff may need to be reflected in higher rates of pay if appropriate staff are to be recruited and retained.

ILF

The Independent Living Fund aims to help severely disabled people who meet its eligibility criteria live in their own homes rather than in residential or nursing care. It aims to enable greater opportunities for choice and control in individual living arrangements; helping to pay the costs of employing one or more assistants to provide personal and domestic care. The Fund works in partnership with local authorities to enable jointly funded packages of care to be arranged.

Applicants must be in receipt of the highest care component of disability living allowance (DLA) and must continue to receive it to remain a client of the Fund. A successful applicant must not have more than £8000 in savings. They must be receiving at least £200 worth of service per week from their local authority social services department.

The Fund cannot pay more than £300 per week. Local authorities cannot use the Fund as a 'top up' in place of its existing commitments. If an individual's needs have changed and the cost of the package will increase, the Fund could become involved but the LA must not reduce its level of financial commitment.

The Fund would not expect to receive applications from people who are being relocated in the community following planned closure of long-stay hospitals.

Summary

1. Financial planning systems within services generally are crude and variable, making it difficult to compare costs across areas and services at a national level

2. Planning circles can help produce outcomes for people that regular services cannot or are not delivering

3. With planning circles, we are likely to see a rise in overall immediate costs associated with the person as more paid staff time goes into facilitating the circle and supporting the goals that result

4. Most of the costs associated with planning circles initiated by the Changing Days project were absorbed within existing resources

5. Using planning circles for all day service users is unlikely to produce savings to the service in the short-term, particularly if day service staff are used as facilitators. But to be meaningful, a long-term view of finances is needed

6. In terms of individuals, there are obvious benefits. Circles are an effective way of supporting and getting to know people with complex needs, and prove cost-effective in terms of the quality of the outcomes and opportunities that result for the person

7. It is important to consider the impact on others in the service. This apparent concentration of resources on the few at the expense of the many may result in a new understanding of where resources are most usefully targeted

8. In many cases, circles were good at involving people from the community, families and paid people from other departments, e.g. leisure

9. Some local authorities have proved successful in securing additional or bridge funding as they have changed services

10. Personal money did not appear to be a barrier to people taking part in community activities

11. Circles produced benefits for people that would be almost impossible to cost but may produce future efficiency savings, e.g. better relationships with carers

12. Many councils are committed to combating social exclusion – this may allow for wider service areas to invest in individuals with learning difficulties

References

1. Kavanagh S, Opit L. *The Cost of Caring – The economics of Providing for the Intellectually Disabled.* London: Politeia, 1998.
2. Flynn M *et al. Taking a Break: Liverpool's respite services for adult citizens with learning disabilities.* Manchester: National Development Team, 1994.
3. Ryan T. *The Cost of Opportunity – Purchasing Strategies in the Housing and Support arrangements of people with learning difficulties.* VIA, 1998.
4. Davis A, Murray J, Flynn M. *Normal Lives? The financial circumstances of people with learning difficulties.* Manchester: National Development Team, 1993.

Further reading

Davies L. *Quality, costs and an 'ordinary life': comparing the costs and quality of different residential services for people with mental handicap.* London: King's Fund, 1987.

Independent Living Fund. *Guidance Notes for 1993 Fund*. Nottingham: ILF, 1994.

Step-by-step from day centres to community

Step-by-step from day centres to community

Raise awareness; what's good about the day service?
What needs to change?

▼

Get agreement from senior managers, elected members, board
members for changes.

▼

Set up a 'change' group to steer the way forward.
Involve users, community members, employers, staff and carers.
Develop a communication strategy which keeps people
informed about and involved with changes.

▼

Staff development to move to a person-centred service which supports
individuals to participate in ordinary activities in an inclusive community.
Undertake person-centred plans (PCPs).
Develop circles of support for each person.

▼

Hold a stakeholders' conference to engage a wide group of people
in the change process and capture their ideas for the future.
Visit examples of innovation and good practice.

▼

Use outcomes from person-centred plans and information from
stakeholders' conference to draft a framework for future services.
Create new job descriptions for staff.

▼

Step-by-step from day centres to community (*cont.*)

Move resources (staffing and finance) to individual support for users (direct payments), invest in supported employment, and community-based opportunities.

Get started on helping people (one-by-one) to participate in new activities, jobs, education opportunities.
Ensure risk assessments are used to minimise problems.

Find new alliances for additional funding (e.g. TEC, Welfare to Work programmes, corporate sponsorship).

Measure improvement in people's lives by looking at original PCPs

Improve opportunities

Appendix 2

Changing Days Personal Planning Book

CHANGING DAYS
PERSONAL PLANNING BOOK

NAME: ....

PERSONAL DETAILS

NAME

AGE

BIRTHDAY

SEX

ADDRESS

TELEPHONE NUMBER

EMERGENCY CONTACT (name and telephone number)

RELIGION

RACE

LANGUAGES SPOKEN AND UNDERSTOOD

DOCTOR

ADVOCATE

WHAT THIS HANDBOOK IS ABOUT

This handbook is to help create a detailed personal plan for the man or woman with learning difficulties you are working with.

As far as possible, it should be 'owned' by the person him/herself. It should be kept close to the person, and should be used when the person is present so that they get to know that it is their property and about them. It should be shared with other people only with the person's agreement.

The questions are written in the first person to help keep attention focused on the person who is at the centre of this plan.

It is important that all the people who know and care about the person (e.g. friends, acquaintances, relatives, day care workers, residential workers) have a chance to contribute to the handbook, either during the course of a planning circle meeting or individually.

Most of the handbook is organised in the following way:

• Left-hand page: questions and explanatory notes for facilitators/supporters
• Right-hand page: space for filling in information

There is space to include drawings, photographs, symbols or anything else visual that you feel is appropriate.

To make it more flexible to use, we strongly advise photocopying the pages and using them in a loose-leaf format. This will allow extra pages to be inserted and sections to be replaced or added to. For example, it may be important to have a version that includes confidential information that only needs to be known by certain people.

Keep in mind that this is an on-going record of the person's life. It will change as the person changes, both as an individual and as their life experiences, activities and relationships change and grow.

ACKNOWLEDGEMENTS
This document is adapted from personal planning material used by:
South & East Belfast Health and Social Services Trust
Ely Hospital, Cardiff
Hackney Social Services and Newham Community NHS Trust,
to whom we extend our grateful thanks.

COMMUNICATION

How do you communicate with others? How do others make themselves understood by you?

The main ways I use to communicate are (e.g. signs, gestures, pictures, symbols, objects, writing):

_____

_____

_____

_____

_____

_____

_____

_____

COMMUNICATION

It is vitally important that everyone who knows the person has a chance to contribute to this section. During the course of the Changing Days work, sharing knowledge of the person very often revealed important details that were hitherto unknown to one or other of the people who had been supporting that individual.

UNDERSTANDING OF SPOKEN LANGUAGE

I understand:

everything you say ☐   short sentences ☐

most sentences ☐   some words, but not sentences ☐

Comments and/or examples

_____

_____

_____

_____

I don't seem to understand any words. I rely on tone of voice, context, etc.

_____

_____

_____

If I don't understand you, I will:_____

_____

_____

_____

If I don't use words, this is the way I tell people what I want, need, feel, understand (e.g. how I indicate YES, NO, PAIN, PLEASURE, etc.):

_____

_____

_____

_____

THE PEOPLE IN MY LIFE

Who are the people you are close to? People in your family? People at work or college? Neighbours and friends? Who are the people you do things with? Talk to? Turn to for help?

Who do you spend the most time with? Who are the people who know you best?

These are the people you might want to invite to your planning circle. They might be able to support you in your plans for the future.

RELATIONSHIP MAP

Anchors:	The people closest to me. People who love me and will be there for me no matter what! People who, regardless of any changes in my life or me or changes in them or their own life, will still be around to care about me and support me.
Allies:	Not as close as anchors, but with whom I have a strong relationship – for example a friend.
Acquaintances:	People who know me but I see or contact less often – e.g. casual friends, neighbours I say hello to, people I know from where I worship.
Associates:	People I know mainly because of their job or role or profession. People who are paid to offer me a service or support me, e.g. doctor, dentist, physiotherapist, solicitor, people who serve me in the corner shop, café, pub.

This section is a key objective of all your work: to get more people into the person's life, particularly ordinary citizens/informal supports outside of special services.

In completing the map, it is important to include EVERYONE the person comes into contact with, including the person at the supermarket checkout, in the corner shop, at the drycleaners, etc. You never know where any of these contacts may lead in the future. Acquaintances may become Allies or even Anchors.

THE PEOPLE IN MY LIFE

RELATIONSHIPS – SOCIAL NETWORKS

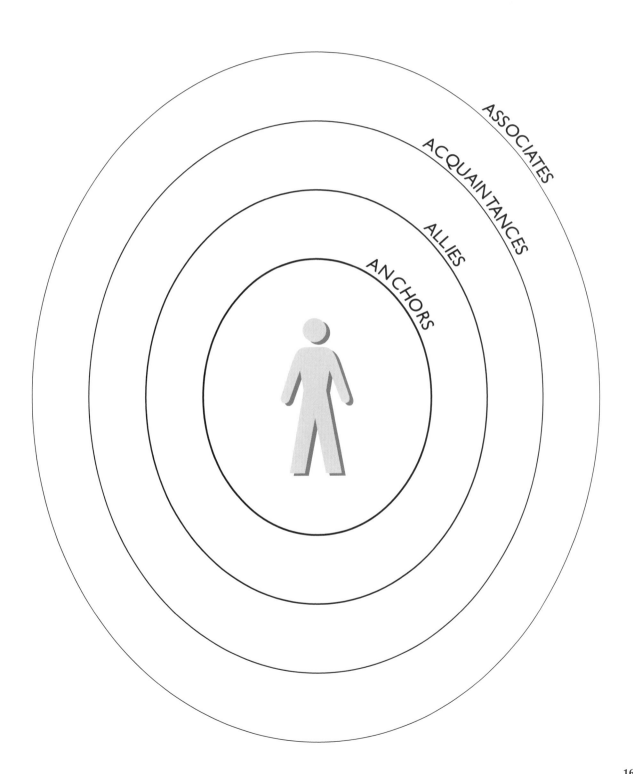

MY LIFE NOW

Think about all the things you do during the week. Fill in the timetable to show what things you do and when you do them.

These are things like going to a day centre, work, college, club, place of worship, visiting family or friends, outings.

MY LIFE NOW

Here we need a picture of what the person usually does in an average week: where they go and what they do there; when they go and for how long. As well as introducing new activities and opportunities the person wants to try, you are aiming to increase the amount of non-segregated activities she/he is involved in.

The following questions may help you decide which current activities might become more inclusive and how you might assist this:

- does it happen in an ordinary setting?
- is it alongside ordinary citizens?
- is it valued by other people?
- does it make best use of the person's skills?
- does it give choice?

WHAT I DO NOW

Name:..

as at: .... (date)

Day & Time	Monday	Tuesday	Wednesday	Thursday	Friday	Saturday	Sunday
A.M.							
P.M.							
Evening							

MY LIFE PATH

A brief story of my life so far. Where I have lived? What I have done? Who have been the important people in my life – present and past? Dates that are important dates to me?

MY LIFE PATH

This section is important for helping to discover old interests, skills once used, long-lost people, connections that might be renewed, e.g.

- where she/he has lived (family home(s), moves to hospital/residential care/group home/supported living)
- family events (birth of brother/sister, death of grandparents, family marriages)
- achievements (e.g. skills learned)
- setbacks (e.g. major illness)
- holidays
- key people – came – went! (e.g. staff the person was close to.)

Each person should have a life history book or portfolio. This not only empowers the individual by giving them a way of knowing about themselves and sharing their experiences with others, but also is an interesting and creative way of producing the material needed for this section.

MY LIFE PATH

Year Born:
19–

WHAT ARE SOME GOOD THINGS ABOUT YOU?
(skills, interests, abilities, personality)

What do you like about yourself? What are you good at? Proud of? What nice things do people say about you?

GOOD THINGS ABOUT ME

You are aiming to build up a complete picture of the individual. Detail is particularly important here. Record everything positive you can think of — even small details.

It should be possible to fill the opposite page with words, phrases, drawings or photos that will give a picture of who the person is.

GOOD THINGS ABOUT ME

WHAT THINGS DO YOU LIKE TO DO?

What things do you like to do? At home? At work? At college? For fun? Around town? On holiday? What kind of music do you like? What kind of films do you like? What kind of food do you like? Do you have any hobbies? Do you belong to any groups or clubs? Do you collect things?

MY LIST OF FAVOURITE THINGS

WHAT THINGS DON'T YOU LIKE?

What things don't you like doing at home? At work? At college? What kinds of food do you not like? What kinds of things upset you, make you angry, sad, annoyed?

THINGS I DON'T LIKE

BEST WEEKDAY

What would be your best weekday? If you could do anything, what would it be? What would you do when you first get up? What would you have for breakfast? What would you have for lunch? What would you do during the day? What kind of activities would you choose? What kind of activities would make you happy?

MY BEST EVENING

What would be your best evening? What would you do when you first get home? What would you have for dinner? What would you do in the time before you go to bed?

MY BEST WEEKEND

What would you do when you first get up? What would you do on Saturday? What would you do on Sunday?

BEST WEEKDAY

WHEN I FIRST GET UP

_____

_____

_____

_____

_____

MY BEST EVENING

WHEN I GET HOME

_____

_____

_____

_____

_____

MY BEST WEEKEND

WHEN I FIRST GET UP

_____

_____

_____

_____

_____

WHAT IS IMPORTANT TO ME

Think about the people who are important in your life, things you like to do, your best day, evening, weekend. What is most important for us to remember? What things do you want to make sure are in your life every day (like a cup of coffee in the morning or a favourite friend)? What things do you want to make sure are not in your life every day (like a certain kind of music or some food you can't stand)?

WHAT IS IMPORTANT TO ME

Here we are prioritising and listing what is important to the person, particularly routines. As Essential Lifestyle Planning describes it:

*   Essentials or non-negotiables
*   Strong preferences
*   Highly desirables

For example:

Relating to pace of life
*   Must not be rushed, must move at his/her own pace, not have others try to move him/her faster
*   Must stay busy; being involved in ......

Relating to routines important to the individual
*   In the morning do not talk to me until after my first coffee
*   When I come home, I must change into my slippers
*   I must ring my mother every evening

THINGS THAT ARE IMPORTANT TO ME

WHERE I LIVE NOW

_____

_____

_____

_____

_____

WHAT I LIKE ABOUT WHERE I LIVE

_____

_____

_____

_____

_____

WHAT I DON'T LIKE ABOUT IT

_____

_____

_____

_____

_____

WHERE I WANT TO LIVE IN THE FUTURE AND WHO WITH

_____

_____

_____

_____

_____

ARE THERE THINGS WE NEED TO KNOW OR DO TO SUPPORT YOU?

Are there things we haven't talked about that would help us support you? For example, are there things we need to know or do to support your health? Are there certain medicines you take?

Are there certain physical things that you should or should not do? Are there certain things we need to know or do to make sure you stay safe? Are there things we need to know about the food you eat? Are there things that make you upset that we need to know about?

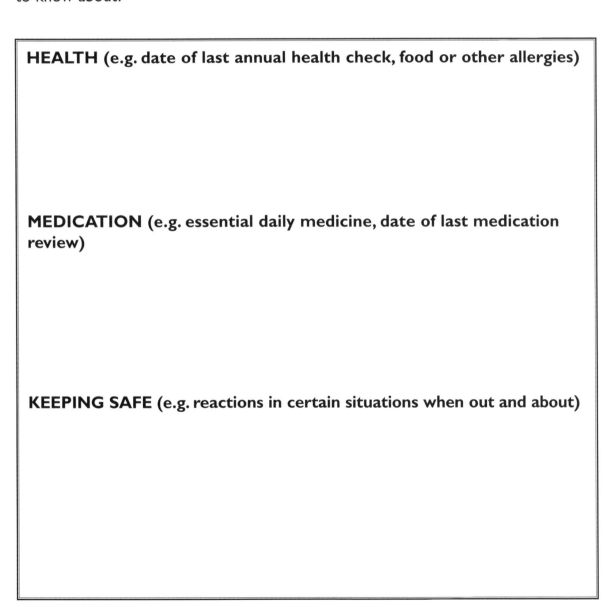

HEALTH (e.g. date of last annual health check, food or other allergies)

MEDICATION (e.g. essential daily medicine, date of last medication review)

KEEPING SAFE (e.g. reactions in certain situations when out and about)

WHAT ARE YOUR DREAMS/HOPES AND WISHES FOR THE FUTURE?

Are there things you would like to be able to do but don't have the chance to do at present, e.g. swimming, work placement, going to college, see your relatives more often, visit a friend, have a holiday in the Bahamas, climb the Himalayas?!

MY DREAMS, HOPES
AND WISHES

MY GOALS

as at (date)................

WITHIN ONE MONTH

_____
_____
_____
_____
_____

WITHIN THREE TO SIX MONTHS

_____
_____
_____
_____
_____

WITHIN ONE YEAR

_____
_____
_____
_____
_____

WITHIN FIVE YEARS

_____
_____
_____
_____
_____

MY ACTION PLAN

as at (date) . . . .

Goal	What is the First Step?	Who Will Do It?	When?	Who/What Else Could Help You?	How Will You Know When You have Achieved the Goal?
Within One Month					
Within Three to Six Months					
Within One Year					

187

PEOPLE IN MY LIFE

Please write below the contact details of the people identified in the relationship map.

NAME	ADDRESS & TELEPHONE NO.

DATES OF CIRCLE MEETINGS

_____

_____

_____

_____

_____

_____

_____

_____

_____

CIRCLE MEMBERS (ADDRESS AND TELEPHONE NO.)

_____

_____

_____

_____

_____

_____

_____

_____

_____

_____

Index